REVISED
HIGHER
AND
INTERMEDIATE 2
HISTORY

OPTION C —Britain 1850s–1979 and the
Growth of Nationalism (Germany / Italy)
& SPECIAL TOPIC on Appeasement
and the Road to War

by

M.L. Gillies

ROBERT GIBSON · Publisher
17 Fitzroy Place, Glasgow, G3 7SF, Scotland, U.K.

PREFACE

This book is not intended as a substitute for text-books. It is designed as a study aid for candidates preparing for History courses at Higher or at Intermediate 2 levels.

Higher Still courses involve both internal and external assessment. The arrangements for Later Modern History include a considerable amount of overlap between Higher and Intermediate 2 in 'popular' content areas.

At Intermediate 2, candidates are required to study three specific contexts, (1) Historical Study: Scottish and British, (2) Historical Study: European and the World, and (3) Historical Study: Optional, whose context is chosen from either (1) or (2). This book covers content in (1) Intermediate Units, From the Cradle to the Grave? Social Welfare in Britain 1890s–1951 or Campaigning for Change: Social Change in Scotland 1900s–1979, and in (2) the following Intermediate Units: Cavour, Garibaldi and the Making of Italy 1815–1870; Iron and Blood? Bismarck and the creation of the German Empire 1815–1871 and the Road to War 1933–1939.

Higher History is made up of three Units, which correspond to Sections A, B and C of this book. (1) Historical Study: Scottish and British: Britain 1850s–1979; (2) Historical Study: European and World: the Growth of Nationalism (Germany or Italy) and (3) Historical Special Topic: Appeasement and the Road to War, to 1939.

Higher candidates are expected to write essays on the first two Units. At the end of each chapter in Sections A and B, there are lists of useful essay titles. The third Unit, the Special Topic, requires candidates to answer questions on source material. This Section on Appeasement and the Road to War is designed to enable the student to relate given sources to the context of the topic.

Finally, both Intermediate 2 and Higher levels require the student, as part of the external assessment, to write an Extended Essay (Higher) or an Extended Response (Intermediate 2) on an issue drawn from one of the Units which have been studied. Should the student wish to select an issue from the Special Topic, a list of useful essay titles is appended at the end of the section on Appeasement and the Road to War. The material in this book will therefore provide suggestions of possible topics for the Extended Essay / Response.

CONTENTS

Section A: Britain 1850–1979

Section B: The Growth of Nationalism

Section C: Special Topic — Appeasement and the Road to War, to 1939

1. THE GROWTH OF DEMOCRACY

One of the main themes of late 19th century and early 20th century Britain was the growth of democracy: one man, one vote; one vote, one value.

The Electoral System Before the Second Reform Act (1867)

Although the 1832 Reform Act had introduced major changes to the electoral system in Britain, it did not introduce democracy. The reform did however show the possibility of non-revolutionary change in the way Britain was governed.

The Act of 1832 (1) increased the franchise and (2) redistributed the constituencies.

1. In county seats the vote was exercised by adult males owning freehold property worth at least 40 shillings (£2) per annum. In addition the better-off tenants were given the vote (they were defined as £10 long-leaseholders and £50 short-leaseholders). In the boroughs there was one qualification — adult males owning or occupying property worth at least £10 per annum. As a result the estimated proportion of adult males in England and Wales entitled to vote increased from 11% to 18% between 1831 and 1833. By 1866, 1,056,659 out of 5,373,033 adult males could vote (20%).

2. The 1832 Act abolished the worst of the rotten boroughs (seats with few voters). It gave extra seats to the counties and the large towns. For example, in Scotland there were now 30 county seats and 23 burgh seats which included 2 members each from Edinburgh and Glasgow, while Dundee, Greenock, Paisley and Perth returned 1 member each.

This system failed to satisfy Radical demands. In particular the Chartist movement, launched in the late 1830s, put forward six points — manhood suffrage, annual elections, abolition of the property qualification for M.Ps, payment of M.Ps, the secret ballot and equal electoral districts.

The Extension of the Franchise

1. *1867 Reform Act*

    This was one of the main changes of Queen Victoria's reign. The extension of the franchise reflected the demand that the working man be given the vote. It was passed by a Conservative government headed by Disraeli, who advocated a 'Tory Democracy' and aimed to end the Whig-Liberal stranglehold on power.

The key change was the extension of the franchise in the boroughs to all male householders. In addition, lodgers who paid £10 p.a. for unfurnished rooms were enfranchised. In the counties the vote was extended to less well-off tenants defined as £12 leaseholders. Each borough with 10,000 inhabitants lost one M.P. and as a result 25 new seats went to the counties and 20 to the towns.

This reform was described as a 'leap in the dark', in that it doubled the electorate, adding nearly one million new voters to the electorate. About a third of the adult male population could now vote. There was now a clear commitment to democracy.

2. *1884 Third Reform Act*

This was passed under Gladstone's Liberal government (1880–85). It abolished the different voting qualifications between county and borough: household suffrage was now the rule everywhere. The new rural voters meant that the majority of adult males had the vote.

The Representation of the People Acts in the 20th Century

The commitment to democracy was fulfilled after the First World War. In 1918, all men over 21 and women over 30 were enfranchised. For the first time, the franchise did not depend on a property qualification. As a result, the Act more than doubled the electorate. The 1928 Act gave women the vote on the same terms as men, while in 1969 all persons over 18 were enfranchised.

Electoral Corruption

The extension of the franchise in 1867 necessitated the prevention of bribery and corruption. So the Ballot Act of 1872 ensured that elections would be conducted fairly and honestly by replacing 'open voting' with a secret ballot.

The elimination of corruption was carried further with the Corrupt Practices Act of 1883. This made corruption in elections punishable by severe fines and limited candidates' election expenses greatly.

Redistribution of Seats Act 1885

This important measure was passed as part of a 'package' agreed by the Conservative and Liberal parties, along with the Third Reform Act. It disfranchised all boroughs with less than 15,000 inhabitants; boroughs with fewer than 50,000 inhabitants were now to return one member only, not two or three as before. The counties and larger boroughs were divided, each returning one member.

The 1918 Representation of the People Act provided for a redistribution of seats, aiming at creating uniform constituencies, each of about 70,000 voters. This approached the Chartist ideal of equal electoral districts.

Changes in Party Organisation

The extension of the electorate forced the political parties to improve their organisations. No longer could candidates know all the voters personally. In 1867, the Conservatives set up the National Union of Conservative Associations and in 1870 Disraeli founded Conservative Central Office. This provided leaflets, speakers and candidates for Conservative associations in the large borough constituencies. Improved organisation helped the Conservatives to victory in the 1874 election. In 1877 the National Liberal Federation was established to improve Liberal party organisation throughout the country. Supported by Joseph Chamberlain, it was designed to give radicals a greater say in Liberal party policy and end aristocratic Whig domination of the party.

There was now less room for independent M.Ps. To attract support, the parties tended to emphasize their differences. The years after 1867 saw a great duel between Gladstone and the Liberals and Disraeli and the Conservatives. Gladstone was the first national political figure to actively campaign in elections addressing large public meetings. For example, in 1879 in the Midlothian campaign, the Liberal leader attacked the Conservative government's record, especially its handling of foreign policy. His example was followed by others including Joseph Chamberlain, Mayor of Birmingham (1873–1876) and M.P. (1876–1906) and Lord Salisbury, the Conservative leader from 1881–1902.

The Problem of the House of Lords

The problem of a non-elected chamber with a permanent Conservative majority faced Liberal governments. In 1893, the Lords rejected the second Home Rule Bill for Ireland. Representing the hereditary peerage, the Lords were an obstacle to the growth of democracy in Britain. After the Liberal landslide victory in the election of 1906, the Conservatives used the House of Lords to block government measures. This culminated in the rejection of the People's budget in 1909 which aimed to finance social reforms and increased naval expenditure through increased taxes on the better-off. Lloyd George led a campaign attacking the Lords which he called 'Mr. Balfour's poodle' (Balfour was the Conservative leader, 1902–1911).

In 1910, there were two General Elections, as a result of which the Lords passed the Parliament Act (1911) under the threat of a mass creation of Liberal Peers. This was a victory for the House of Commons and for the representatives of the people over the peerage. It required there to be a general election every five years, not seven as previously; it deprived the Lords of power over bills to raise national taxation; and it abolished the Lords' veto over other Bills and replaced it by a delaying power of two years.

Women's Suffrage

One of the greatest changes in the 20th century is the changed status of women in society. In the early years of the 20th century, feminist activity centred round the struggle for the vote.

'Votes for Women'

J.S. Mill, the Liberal M.P., proposed in 1867 an amendment to Disraeli's Reform Bill substituting 'person' for 'men'. The rejection of this motion spurred the formation of a number of women's suffrage societies. In 1897, a number of these societies amalgamated in the National Union of Women's Suffrage Societies (N.U.W.S.S.). These 'suffragists', led by Mrs. Millicent Fawcett, believed in peaceful persuasion to achieve their objectives. These were to seek the vote for women 'as it is, and may be given to men'. This side-stepped the controversial question of adult suffrage at a time when not all men were enfranchised. Thus the N.U.W.S.S. avoided the democratic demand for adult suffrage. By 1914, the N.U.W.S.S. had some 53,000 members and over 480 branches.

7

The 1867 and 1884 Reform Acts, by enfranchising the majority of men, served to highlight the fact that sex had become the outstanding disqualification. Moreover, women were allowed to vote in local government elections. The 1869 Municipal Franchise Act allowed single women ratepayers to vote in municipal elections. Propertied women could vote for School Boards (1870), Poor Law Boards (1875), County Councils (1888) and Parish and District Councils (1894). Women also established the right to be elected to these bodies.

What were the various arguments used to oppose women's suffrage?

1. It was argued that a woman's husband could perform political functions on her behalf.

2. A woman's role centred on marriage, child-bearing and the domestic.

3. Women were alleged to be emotional and trivial.

4. Many M.Ps disliked the prospect of women M.Ps.

5. Women lacked physical strength and so could not fight for their country, an argument often advanced by imperialists.

The Suffragettes.

Public attention to the question of women's suffrage was the result of the suffragette campaign, led by Mrs. Emmeline Pankhurst. In 1903, she formed the Women's Social and Political Union (W.S.P.U.) which at first adopted similar tactics to the N.U.W.S.S. — education of the public on the subject of female suffrage. However, the failure of the Liberal government to act provoked a militant campaign from 1905 onwards. They interrupted Liberal party meetings, chained themselves to railings, smashed windows and attacked government ministers. Up to 1908 this seemed to pay dividends — it brought the suffrage question to national attention. After 1909, however, militancy got out of hand. Many suffragettes went on hunger-strike in prison and were forcibly fed. In 1912, they started to set fire to pillar-boxes and in 1913 went in for widespread arson. That same year, Emily Davison, a member of the W.S.P.U., threw herself in front of the King's horse at the Derby and died of her injuries. The 'Cat and Mouse' Act of 1913 enabled the authorities to release prisoners whose health was endangered by hunger-strike and then re-arrest them. The evidence suggests that the campaign did more harm than good to the cause of women's suffrage. Politicians and the public turned against the W.S.P.U. Mrs. Pankhurst ruled the W.S.P.U.

dictatorially and offended many supporters. Far from winning public opinion, the W.S.P.U. lost it.

Why did women's suffrage not come sooner?

The Liberal government of 1906–1914 had to bear the brunt of the suffragette campaign. The government had more pressing priorities than votes for women — including social reforms, the struggle with the House of Lords and the Irish problem. Moreover, the issue could not be separated from party advantage. All three parties, Conservative, Liberal and Labour, were divided on this problem. In particular, many Liberals opposed enfranchising only propertied women on the grounds that they were Conservatives. It therefore had to be universal suffrage for both sexes or nothing. This helps to explain the failure of Bills between 1910 and 1912, drawn up by an all-party Commons committee to enfranchise women property owners. These Bills failed to pass because many Liberals and Labour were opposed to limited women's suffrage. The suffragettes were infuriated: they did not mind how few women were enfranchised as long as the principle was established. The Labour party was not keen on an enfranchisement which did not introduce adult suffrage, as it would be a betrayal of the working class. As often in the suffragette campaign, women's suffrage was equated exclusively with wealthy and propertied women.

Conclusion

It is often said that the work of women during the First World War brought them the vote. There is little doubt that women played an important part in the war effort and that this was one factor in gaining the vote in 1918. Between 1914 and 1918, the number of women employed in Britain rose by 1,345,000 as a result of the need for substitutes for men drawn into the armed forces. Women worked in munitions factories, banking, clerical work, the civil service, nursing, transport and agriculture. The politicians were prepared in the 1918 Representation of the People Act to find a compromise without however conceding equal franchise. Thus women who were occupiers or the wives of occupiers, with a minimum age of 30, could vote. Women had been patriotic and it would be churlish to deny them the vote — provided they stayed in the minority. There were six men to every four women in the new electorate. Critics pointed to the fact that many women who contributed to the war effort such as the munitions girls were under 30 and still without the vote.

In the years which followed, the absence of obvious political differences between men and women facilitated progress towards equalisation of the franchise. In 1928, with little opposition, Baldwin's Conservative government secured an Equal Franchise Bill sweeping away the age limitation. It added five and a quarter million women to the register in time for the 1929 election; they now comprised 52·7% of the total.

Essay Questions to Consider

1. What progress did Britain make towards becoming a democracy between 1850 and 1914?

2. To what extent had democracy been achieved in Britain by 1900?

3. How representative of the people was parliament by (a) 1885 and (b) 1914?

4. Which factors contributed most to the extension of the franchise between 1860 and 1928?

5. Why was there a growth in democracy in Britain between 1860 and 1918?

6. To what extent did the widening of the franchise change British politics between 1850 and 1928?

7. Why did it take so long for women to win the vote?

8. Did militancy help or hinder women's struggle for political equality in the years before the First World War?

9. How important a part did events during the First World War play in the decision to grant women the vote?

10. "By 1928 democracy had been achieved." How far do you agree?

2. THE LIBERAL SOCIAL REFORMS

The Origins of the Liberal Welfare Reforms, 1906–1914

In the history of social policy in Britain, the years 1906–1914 stand out as one of the periods of major reform. Old Age Pensions, insurance against ill-health and unemployment, school meals and medical services for children were introduced. Minimum wages were fixed in certain industries. Why was there such a concentrated burst of activity by the Liberal governments of these years?

The social reforms seemed to run counter to the *laissez-faire* individualist ideology of the 19th century Liberal party. This held to the view that the less state regulation the better. The Liberal party won a landslide victory in the 1906 election on the basis, not of a programme of social reform, but in defence of Free Trade. This was a traditional Liberal policy which was challenged by the Unionists' adoption of tariff reform or protection as a response to the rise of foreign competition. The Liberals' success was due to the identification in the public mind of Free Trade with cheap food.

For a variety of reasons it seems likely that whichever party had won the 1906 election, a number of social reforms would have been passed. There were changing attitudes to poverty. Instead of moral judgements which attributed poverty to idleness or drunkenness, there was increasing acceptance of economic and environmental explanations. Around 1900, a series of social enquiries showed the extent of poverty in Britain. In particular, the social surveys of Booth and Rowntree helped to change attitudes. **Charles Booth**, a wealthy shipowner, carried out between 1886 and 1903 an immense investigation, published in 17 volumes, of *The Life and Labour of the People of London*. Booth's sources of information included the Census, School Board attendance officers' reports, interviews with Poor Law Boards of Guardians, teachers, police, sanitary inspectors, trade union officials, charity workers and clergy. He was assisted by a talented team including Beatrice Webb. His original intention was to disprove what he considered to be exaggerated estimates of the extent of poverty in London. In fact, his findings confirmed the extent of poverty. Booth showed that 30% of the capital's population was below the 'poverty line' — a minimum income of between 18 and 21 shillings a week for a family with 3 children. Thus nearly a third of the people of London did not have an income sufficient to maintain the most frugal mode of life. Booth's work stimulated others to analyse social conditions. **Seebohm Rowntree's** *Poverty: A Study of Town Life* (1901) was

11

influenced by Booth's work. Rowntree, of the chocolate firm, investigated his own city of York. Taking up Booth's idea of the 'poverty line', he went on to distinguish between 'primary' poverty and 'secondary' poverty. Primary poverty existed where income was insufficient to meet basic needs; secondary poverty, where income was sufficient, but misspent so as to produce poverty. He identified the main causes of 'primary' poverty as low wages, large families, unemployment, old age or the death of the chief wage earner. His findings that nearly 28% of York's population were in poverty confirmed Booth's figures for London.

Public conscience was also shocked by the fact that 34% of recruits for military service in the **Boer War (1899–1902)** failed to meet the army's standards of height, weight and eyesight: a rejection rate of one in three. The Boer War led to a campaign for **'national efficiency'** which flourished at the turn of the century. This reflected concern at the slower growth of the economy and the relative decline in industrial production compared with Germany and the U.S.A. Politicians like Joseph Chamberlain and Lord Rosebery expressed this concern. It was argued that national efficiency and imperial strength required a better educated and healthier population. Welfare services would contribute to the efficiency of workers. The idea of national efficiency became part of the language of the time and many found it reasonable to express their support for social measures in such terms.

Foreign influences were also important in the introduction of social reforms. Germany in the 1880s had launched a system of sickness and accident insurance. In 1898, New Zealand had introduced old age pensions. Booth supported state pensions, while Lloyd George visited Germany in 1908 where he had seen for himself the German scheme of sickness insurance.

Another influence is the change of opinion often referred to as the **rise of 'collectivism'**, i.e. a more positive role for the state in an individualist society. This influenced Liberals like Asquith, Lloyd George and Churchill and amounted to a 'New Liberalism' which tried to reconcile individualism and social justice. This was a reflection of the rise of socialism seen in the growth of the trade unions and of the new Labour Party. The Labour Movement was calling for old age pensions and for action against unemployment. The Liberals had to keep an eye on the Labour threat and so deal with social questions. Indeed both Liberals and Unionists were under pressure to take account of working class wishes. They faced a common challenge from Labour and many regarded social reform as an antidote to socialism. Thus the pressure on the Liberals to introduce social reforms would have been felt by any government at this time. Where the two differed was over how to finance social reforms; the Liberals favoured direct taxation, while the Unionists preferred to pay for them out of protectionist duties.

Liberal Social Reforms, 1906 – 1914

By 1914 the Liberal government had passed a number of very important social reforms. The details of these measures were as follows.

1. *The Young*

   Concern over the health of the young led to the provision of school meals for needy children in 1906. The following year saw the introduction of school medical inspection. In 1908, juvenile courts and Borstals, as an alternative to prison for young persons, were established.

2. *The Old*

   Old Age Pensions had long been proposed. Charles Booth's investigations of poverty in London convinced him that it was often the result of old age. In 1908, the government introduced a non-contributory scheme for the payment of five shillings a week to those over 70. Pensions were paid at the Post Office and so escaped the stigma of poor relief payments. The amount was small and it was not intended to replace savings.

3. *In and Out of Work*

   In 1908, miners secured an eight-hour day, the first time the length of the working day was fixed for adult men. In 1909, the Trade Boards Act tried to protect workers in the sweated trades like tailoring and lace making by setting up trade boards to determine minimum wages and maximum hours. In 1911, the Shops Act made compulsory for shop assistants a weekly half day off.

   In 1909, Labour Exchanges were set up to provide information on available jobs. The climax of the Liberal social reforms was the National Insurance Act of 1911. Compulsory insurance against unemployment in trades where it was likely was introduced for the benefit of about two and a quarter million workers, including building and engineering workers. Employer, employee and the state made weekly contributions to the insurance fund. This provided seven shillings a week for a maximum of 15 weeks. This scheme was expanded enormously between the wars in the face of large-scale unemployment.

Health insurance was also introduced in the 1911 Act. Much poverty was the result of sickness. The author of the scheme, Lloyd George, visited Germany in 1908, where he saw the German scheme of insurance against sickness. Everyone earning up to £160 per annum was compulsorily insured against ill-health. The employer and employee made weekly contributions, as did the state. The insured man received ten shillings a week when off sick for up to 26 weeks and free medical care from a doctor. The scheme did not cover the other members of the employee's family, who still had to pay doctor's bills. Yet the later N.H.S. owes much to this scheme.

Assessment of the Liberal Social Reforms

These Liberal reforms were the greatest body of social legislation passed by any one government up to that time. The 1909 People's Budget proposed to pay the cost of the new pension scheme by increasing income tax and death duties and imposing a super-tax on high incomes.

The reforms were limited, e.g. Old Age Pensions were inadequate in amount; health insurance covered only the insured and not his family; unemployment insurance was for seven trades only. Yet while this was not a comprehensive welfare state, it laid the foundations of later more comprehensive measures. The Liberal reforms increased state interference on behalf of the population, e.g. Old Age Pensions were non-contributory; insurance against unemployment was compulsory for two and a quarter million workers and against sickness for all earning up to £160 p.a. These social reforms amounted to a 'New Liberalism' more positive than Gladstonian Liberalism, since it united a concern for the freedom of the individual with a willingness to use the power of the state in the interests of the people.

Essay Questions to Consider

1. To what extent did the Liberal Government (1906–1914) set up a welfare state in Britain?

2. "More a product of political necessity than of social concern." It this a fair judgement on the social reforms of the Liberal Government 1906–1914?

3. "Between 1906 and 1914 the real causes of poverty were tackled successfully by government action." To what extent would you agree with this statement?

4. To what extent were the Liberal Social Reforms (1906–1914) prompted by feelings of genuine concern for the masses?

5. To what extent were the Liberals' Social and Trade Union Reforms a response to the growth of the Labour movement between 1906 and 1914?

6. "Their intention was never to lay the foundations of a welfare state but simpy to provide specific solutions to specific social problems." How far do you agree with this assessment of the Liberals' Social Reforms?

7. Would you agree that "there was a marked change in attitude and policies towards poverty and social problems in Britain in the first decade of the 20th century"?

8. "They were prompted by a ground-swell of social pity." Is this an adequate explanation for the introduction of a programme of social reforms in the period 1906–1914?

3. THE LABOUR MOVEMENT TO 1939

The British Labour Movement before 1914

Lib-Labs

The Second Reform Act of 1867 had been the first step in the enfranchise-ment of the working classes. 1868 saw the meeting of the first Trades Union Congress which became the 'voice' of organised labour. In 1874, two working men gained seats in Parliament and became known as Lib-Labs. It was under this label that a few Trade Unionists made their appearance in later Parliaments.

Trade Union Gains

Trade Unionism did not become a mass movement until the end of the 19th century. In 1850, Union membership was probably under 250,000 and was confined mainly to skilled workers. These unions acted like friendly societies dealing with sickness and accident payments and tended to avoid strikes as likely to reduce their funds.

In the 1870s, the Trade Unions made important progress. In 1871, Gladstone's first government gave union funds full legal protection, while in 1875 the Disraeli government allowed peaceful picketing.

'New Unions'

Between the end of the 1880s and 1914, there was a considerable increase in Trade Union membership. This followed a series of publicised strikes, involving unskilled workers. One was a successful strike by match-girls in the East End of London who worked in dreadful conditions; another involved a union of London gas workers who got the working-day cut from twelve hours to eight. This encouraged the dock workers, who were organised into a union by Ben Tillett in 1889. The London dock workers came out demanding sixpence an hour, the 'docker's tanner'. The dockers had no funds but won public support and the employers yielded.

This gave a fillip to trade unionism, notably among unskilled workers. Between 1889 and 1892 the number of trade unionists rose from three quarters of a million to one and a half million. These 'new unions' were less concerned with friendly society activities and more with attempts to improve wages. They were general unions, i.e. they were not confined to certain crafts but included most of those engaged in an industry.

The Origins of the Labour Party

Socialist Groups

In the 1880s, socialist ideas became important in Britain for the first time. Thus in 1884 the Social Democratic Federation (S.D.F.) was formed. This was the first Marxist group in Britain — it was led by H.M. Hyndman — but it was small and mainly confined to middle class intellectuals. The Fabian Society was also founded in 1884. The Fabians aimed to spread socialist ideas among the public and work out the application of socialist principles to British society. The Fabians rejected revolutionary tactics, favouring peaceful evolution. They included the famous writers George Bernard Shaw and Beatrice and Sidney Webb.

The Independent Labour Party

In 1893, the Scottish socialist, Keir Hardie, a Lanarkshire miner's son, who refused to cooperate with the Liberals and had been elected an independent Labour M.P. for West Ham in 1892, took the lead in the formation of an Independent Labour Party. This followed a conference in Bradford attended by some trade unions, the S.D.F., the Fabian Society and the Scottish Labour Party which Hardie had founded in 1888. The I.L.P. was independent of the Liberals and had a socialist programme. However the I.L.P. was short of funds and the T.U.C. held aloof, since Lib-Lab arrangements were still important. In the 1895 election, the I.L.P. failed to secure the election of a single candidate.

The Labour Representation Committee

In 1895, the Liberal party suffered an electoral reverse. The Liberals failed to adopt policies to attract many working class voters, partly because of their obsession with Irish Home Rule. The Liberals had also shown a reluctance to adopt working men as candidates. Therefore, to secure representation in Parliament for the Labour movement, a Labour Representation Committee was formed in 1900. This followed a T.U.C. initiative and a conference in London attended by delegates from the I.L.P., the S.D.F., the Fabian Society and representatives from a number of unions. Ramsay MacDonald was appointed the L.R.C's secretary. In the 1900 election however, only two L.R.C. candidates were elected, including Keir Hardie. Only a few trade unions were affiliated to it.

The Taff Vale Case

What improved the L.R.C's prospects was the Taff Vale case. This was a legal decision resulting from a strike on the Taff Vale Railway in South Wales in 1900, supported by the Amalgamated Society of Railway Servants. The House of Lords found the union liable for civil damages for losses of the railway company caused by the strike. This alarmed the unions because it appeared that when a union supported a strike, it might be made liable for an employer's losses. So there was increased union support for the L.R.C. with the aim of getting the Taff Vale decision reversed. In 1903, MacDonald secured an electoral pact with Herbert Gladstone, the Liberal Chief whip, whereby the two parties agreed not to oppose each other in a number of constituencies. In the 1906 Election, this paid dividends with the return of 29 Labour M.Ps. The L.R.C. now changed its name to the Labour Party.

Labour and the Liberal Government 1906–1914

In 1906, the Liberal government passed the Trade Disputes Act which gave trade unions immunity against actions for damages for losses incurred by employers during a strike. This reversed the Taff Vale decision.

The next legal decision unfavourable to the trade unions was the Osborne Judgement in 1909. Osborne objected to his union spending part of their funds to assist the Labour party. The House of Lords upheld Osborne's complaint. This dealt a blow to Labour party finances and especially subsidies given to Labour M.P.s who did not receive a salary. The two elections of 1910 deprived the Liberal government of its overall majority and forced it to depend on the Irish Nationalists and Labour (which won 42 M.Ps in December 1910). So in 1911 the government secured the payment of M.Ps of £400 p.a. Moreover in 1913 a Trade Union Act was passed whereby unions were allowed to use their funds to support a political party, any member objecting to part of his subscription going into the political fund being entitled to 'contract out'. It must be remembered that prior to 1914, the Labour Party was subordinate to the Liberal government with, as yet, no prospect of securing power in its own right.

Labour Militancy Before 1914

The years 1910–1914 saw serious Labour unrest. Many days were lost in strikes. For example, in 1911 there were dock strikes in London and Liverpool; in 1912 a national miners' strike involved the demand for a national minimum wage; 1914 saw the formation of a 'Triple Alliance' of railwaymen, miners and transport workers, involving the threat of sympathy strikes to assist each other. Trade Union membership increased rapidly from 2,500,000 in 1910 to over four million in 1914. At this time unemployment was low and the newly organised workers were in a position to take part in strikes. Labour unrest was also due to falling real wages at a time of rising prices. In addition, some militants were converts to syndicalism, i.e. workers' control of industry and the idea of a general strike.

The Labour Movement Between the Wars

The First World War brought increased influence for Labour. Trade union membership increased from 4 million to 6·5 million by 1918. During the war there was an increase in state control of the economy. Such a development was in line with Labour attitudes. Trade unions were closely consulted by government and management to ensure efficient war production. Some Labour M.Ps, including Arthur Henderson, were brought into the wartime Coalition government.

Industrial Unrest and the General Strike

The post-war strike wave

After 1918, the end of government controls led to rapid price rises and a series of bitter industrial disputes. The pre-war Triple Alliance of miners, railway and transport workers was reformed. Strikes occurred in many industries. There were more strikes in the immediate post-war years than at any other time in the inter-war period, apart from the year of the General Strike. By 1920 there were 8·5 million Trade Unionists. In 1921, 85 million working days were lost through stoppages. Left-wing ideas flourished under the influence of the Bolshevik Revolution in Russia. In Glasgow, troops had to police 'Red Clydeside' in 1919. The post-war strike wave reflected the demand for employers to recognise unions, and for wage increases at a time of rising prices.

The General Strike

From 1921, many unions were on the defensive. Britain's staple industries of cotton, coal, steel and shipbuilding faced increased competition from abroad and found it difficult to maintain exports. Employers sought wage reductions to enable them to cut prices.

The coal industry was at the centre of events leading to the General Strike. It faced a loss of export markets; the industry was out-of-date due to a lack of mechanisation and of coal-cutting machines. Rather than new investment, the owners proposed lower wages and longer hours.

The French occupation of the Ruhr in 1923 eased the problems of the coal industry for a time, as German competition was removed for 18 months (the German mines there were closed during the French occupation). The withdrawal of the French from the Ruhr renewed the slump in exports which were also hit by the return to the Gold Standard in 1925. This increased the value of the pound and imposed a burden on the export industries.

Both the miners and the mineowners were stubborn. Lord Birkenhead said he would have called the miners' leaders the stupidest men in the country had he not had to deal with the owners. The Miners' Federation rejected the Samuel Report (1926). This Inquiry had been appointed by Baldwin's government in 1925 which at the same time provided a temporary subsidy to keep wages at existing levels. This concession followed 'Red Friday' in July 1925, when in the face of wage cuts imposed by the coal owners, the T.U.C. pledged full support to the Miners' Federation, even to the length of a general sympathetic strike. The Samuel Report recommended a reorganisation of the coal industry, though it also proposed an end to the subsidy and temporary reduction in wages. The Miners' Secretary, A.J. Cook, summed up the miners' response, "Not a penny off the pay, not a second on the day". The mine owners too refused to accept the report.

The Idea of a General Strike

This idea was not new. Before the war, the threat of something like it was implied in the formation of the Triple Alliance of miners, railwaymen and transport workers in 1914. The idea was that the three would act together in making wage agreements. In 1925, the T.U.C. General Council had backed the miners in 'Red Friday'. The feeling grew in government circles that a showdown must take place with the trade unions. The government made preparations for a general strike, so that food supplies and transport would continue. The T.U.C. hoped for a settlement right up until the Cabinet broke off negotiations when the *Daily Mail* printers refused to print an article hostile to a general strike. Chancellor Churchill wanted a fight and the Home Secretary, Joynson-Hicks, asked, "Is England to be governed by Parliament and the Cabinet or by a handful of Trade Union leaders?".

When the mine-owners announced wage reductions, the miners went on strike. This was followed by the General Strike which lasted only nine days. The T.U.C. was prepared to seek a compromise on the lines of the Samuel Report but the miners resisted all wage reductions. The government was not prepared to give in and sought the surrender of the T.U.C. Government preparations to meet the General Strike worked well as volunteers drove trains and buses and kept food supplies moving. So, despite the impressive show of working class solidarity, with around three million trade unionists on strike in the railway, transport, steel, building and printing industries, the T.U.C. called off the strike as neither the government nor the miners would give way. The miners remained on strike until they were forced back by the exhaustion of their resources.

The Consequences of the General Strike

After 1926, all talk of a General Strike vanished. 1926 was a set-back to the unions which lost membership. The miners were driven back to work after six months by starvation and were forced to accept lower wages and longer hours. The Miners' Federation was weakened by a 'non-political' union in the Nottinghamshire coalfields. The mining industry was not reorganised (that came only with nationalisation in 1947).

The Conservatives passed the Trade Disputes Act in 1927, declaring all general sympathetic strikes illegal. The funds of a union engaging in an illegal strike were made liable to civil damages. Civil servants were forbidden to join a union affiliated to the T.U.C. Union members who wished to pay the political levy (which financed the Labour party) had to 'contract in', instead of 'contracting out'. This adversely affected the income of the Labour party and angered the Labour movement. The Act was repealed by the Labour government in 1946.

The 1930s saw a decline in union militancy, largely due to high unemployment. The unions were weakened in funds and membership and were forced to fight an uphill battle to protect wages and conditions during the worst phase of the depression. By 1933, union membership had fallen to 4·4 million, less than a quarter of the workforce. By 1939, this had recovered to 6·3 million with the economic revival of the mid and late 1930s. During World War Two the unions recovered much of the ground lost in the Depression and important union leaders like Ernest Bevin were brought into government. After the General Strike episode, organised Labour sought to advance the interests of the workers within the existing economic and political structure, rather than support revolutionary action.

The Two Labour Governments Between the Wars

In 1918, the Labour Party was overhauled with the adoption of a new constitution. This enabled the party for the first time to have individual members and local constituency branches (previously it had been an association of trade unions and socialist organisations like the Fabian Society and the I.L.P.). The party's commitment to socialism was strengthened through Clause 4 of the constitution calling for the 'common ownership of the means of production'. Also in 1918, S. Webb drafted a new party programme, 'Labour and the New Social Order', calling for nationalisation, the maintenance of full employment through public works and more redistributive taxation. Just after the Armistice, the party withdrew support from the Coalition so as to fight the General Election in its own right.

Before 1914, the Labour Party was rather like a pressure group and was largely supportive of the Liberal governments of 1906–1914. After 1918, Liberal divisions between the supporters of Lloyd George and Asquith allowed the Labour Party to become the viable alternative Opposition to the Conservatives. Labour was no longer dependent on the Liberals and the party now had its own distinctive organisation and policies.

Labour was also assisted by the 1918 Representation of the People Act which gave the vote to a further two million working class men as well as enfranchising six million women. Many of the new voters were likely to support Labour. In 1922, Labour made a major breakthrough, becoming the official Opposition for the first time, after it had won more seats than the Liberals. In the election of 1923, Labour was again ahead of the Liberals, even though the two sections of Liberals were reunited. The following year, Labour formed a government under Ramsay MacDonald. This first Labour government lacked a parliamentary majority and was dependent on Liberal support in the Commons. There was therefore no question of introducing radical measures to redistribute wealth.

Although the Labour government was short-lived, it was clear by 1924 that Labour had replaced the Liberals as the alternative party of government to the Conservatives. Despite its brevity, the first Labour government proved a Labour government could work.

The Fall of the First Labour Government

In October 1924, MacDonald resigned after a defeat in the House of Commons. This followed an adverse vote on the government's refusal to prosecute J.R. Campbell, editor of the *Communist Workers' Weekly*, who had urged soldiers not to fire on workers in a strike. During the election which followed, the *Daily Mail* published the 'Zinoviev Letter', which purported to be from the Soviet Communist Party to the British Communist Party (which had been founded in 1920 in the aftermath of the Russian Revolution). This letter involved advice on how to organise a revolution. MacDonald's government had given diplomatic recognition to the Soviet regime and had signed a trade treaty with it. The Zinoviev Letter was alleged to show that Labour was encouraging the British Communists.

The Second Labour Government (1929–1931)

The failure of the General Strike seemed to indicate to the Labour movement the futility of using large-scale industrial action against a determined Conservative government: it was better to concentrate on political action. In the 1929 election, the Conservatives were defeated. They lost over 140 seats and for the first time Labour was the largest party, winning 288 seats to the Conservatives' 260. However, Labour still lacked an overall majority, as the Liberals had 59 seats. The Conservative defeat reflected continuing high levels of unemployment and bitterness over the General Strike. The Conservatives' slogan, 'Safety First', seemed dull and uninspiring.

23

MacDonald's second administration was overwhelmed by the world economic crisis, following the Wall Street crash in October 1929. World trade fell and unemployment rose. In Britain it reached 2·5 million by December 1930. This in turn led to mounting government expenditure on unemployment benefit.

One of MacDonald's ministers, Sir Oswald Mosley, grew disillusioned at the failure of his colleagues to tackle unemployment and in 1930 produced a Memorandum — a programme of economic reconstruction including a government-financed plan of public works, import restrictions, subsidies to farmers, earlier pensions and a later school-leaving age. He resigned when his advice was rejected and in 1932 founded the British Union of Fascists.

In 1931, the financial crisis deepened as a result of bank failures in Germany and Austria and diminishing gold reserves in Britain. In July the Report of the all-party May Committee, set up by the P.M. to report on the nation's finances, was published. It forecast a large deficit and proposed cuts in public expenditure by reductions in public-sector wages and in unemployment benefit. The Labour government broke up over the question of reducing unemployment benefit. The P.M. and a few colleagues were prepared to implement the cuts but they lacked the agreement of their colleagues and resigned.

Instead of returning to Opposition, MacDonald agreed to form a National Government with the Conservatives and Liberals. For this he was condemned as a traitor to the Labour movement and expelled from the party. In the 1931 election, called by the National government, the Labour party suffered an almost complete rout, being reduced to 52 seats, fewer than in 1918. The party was divided and in disarray.

In the 1935 election, Labour put forward a programme of nationalisation and comprehensive social services. The results were à bitter disappointment. Though the party won back some 100 seats, the National Government with 432 M.Ps retained an enormous majority. There was as yet no confidence in an alternative Labour government. It was to take another world war and a major change in national opinion before Labour would be given power to implement its policies.

So the two inter-war Labour governments were a disappointment to their supporters. Why were they not more successful?

1. Both were minority governments dependent on Liberal votes to stay in office. It was therefore out of the question to introduce nationalisation or radical measures of wealth redistribution and their policies differed little from those of Liberal governments.

2. The Labour Party depended on the trade unions for most of its funds. Union leaders expected to control the party and were critical of 'half-measures'. There were unsuccessful attempts by some trade unionists to have the party forbidden to participate in minority governments. The government of 1924 had strained relations with the unions following strikes by dockers and London transport workers.

3. Both Labour governments faced serious economic problems; one million unemployed in 1924 and the 1930–1931 world economic crisis. Labour had no answer beyond nationalisation which was out of the question for a minority government.

5. MacDonald offended the Left of his party by accepting the limitations of minority government and failing to bring in genuine socialist measures which, if defeated in the Commons, could enable Labour to appeal to the electorate. MacDonald wanted moderate policies to gain the confidence of the country. His critics decided that he was no socialist.

After 1931, MacDonald's position was difficult as he was backed by only a tiny National Labour group in the House of Commons. He was a 'man without a party', as the Conservatives dominated Parliament. He was in effect their prisoner and in 1935, with failing eyesight and ill-health, gave way to Baldwin as P.M.

Essay Questions to Consider

1. "The Labour Party was set up not so much to represent the working class as to represent the Trade Unions." Do you agree?

2. Account for the emergence of the Labour Party at the beginning of the 20th century and assess its electoral success by 1914.

3. How important was the contribution of the socialist societies to the growth of the Labour Movement in Britain up to 1914?

4. How important a role did the Trade Unions play in the development of the Labour Party by 1914?

5. How significant were the advances made by the trade union movement between 1900 and 1914?

6. How significant was the support of the Trade Union movement in the rise of the Labour Party between 1890 and 1924?

7. How big an impact did the Labour Movement have on British politics and society by 1924?

8. To what extent can the British Labour Party be regarded as a major political force in the inter-war period?

9. Examine the causes and consequences of the General Strike.

10. Did Ramsay MacDonald betray the Labour Party in 1931?

11. How significant a force was the Labour Party in British politics and government between 1919 and 1939?

12. How important was the General Strike for the Trade Union movement?

13. Why did the General Strike fail and what were the consequences of that failure?

14. Account for the formation of the first Labour government in 1924.

4. THE NATIONAL GOVERNMENT AND THE PROBLEMS OF MASS UNEMPLOYMENT AND DEPRESSION

The British Economy Between the Wars

In 1914, Britain's economy seemed strong. Britain was a major producer of coal, steel, textiles and ships. The country was also a major international creditor. However there was a dependence on these 'staple' industries and on their exports.

The Great War involved the expenditure of £11,325 million, much of which was borrowed from the U.S. Thus Britain emerged from the war as a debtor nation. Moreover the war had disrupted Britain's export trade. Overseas markets were lost to industrial rivals like Japan and the U.S. and through the substitution by traditional customers of home-produced for British goods. After a short-lived post-war boom fuelled by rising prices, a slump began in 1920 with the beginnings of a rise in unemployment which reached two million by 1921. This reflected the contraction of the old 'staples' which dominated the inter-war economy and brought with it the problem of persistent mass unemployment.

These industries faced strong foreign competition and a more unsettled international economy. The Wall Street Crash of 1929 led to a profound depression in which world trade fell by 35% between 1929 and 1933. In 1931, a major financial crisis forced Britain off the Gold Standard. (In 1925, Britain, having come off the Gold Standard to finance the war, returned to it with the effect of over-valuing the currency and making exports less competitive.) Steel, shipbuilding, coal and textiles faced great falls in production, though there was a recovery from the mid-1930s.

Yet that is not the whole story of the economy in the inter-war years. There was growth in new sectors. Most striking was the electrical supply industry. By 1933, the national grid was virtually complete. Output of electricity grew four-fold between 1925 and 1939, in spite of the slump. By 1939, two out of three houses had been wired up for electricity. Industry increasingly used electricity as a source of power and many domestic electrical appliances were manufactured, including vacuum cleaners, refrigerators, radios, gramophones and washing machines.

The motor-vehicle industry also expanded. This became a major industry employing around 400,000 people by the end of the 1930s, using mass-production techniques. The industry was concentrated in the Midlands and the London area. The manufacture of aircraft was another part of the development of engineering.

27

The chemical industry was a major growth industry (I.C.I. was established in 1926), producing fertilisers, pharmaceutical goods and artificial fibres like nylon. The construction industry also grew and was engaged in both public and private building.

In the 1930s, it was the old industries — cotton, shipbuilding, coal and steel — which suffered the worst effects of the Depression. They were concentrated on Clydeside, Tyneside and in Cumbria, Lancashire, Ulster and South Wales. By contrast, the Midlands and the South of England suffered less and enjoyed a degree of prosperity after 1934. These were the areas where the 'new' industries were being established. Baldwin's decisive victory in the 1935 election was the result of this economic revival which was assisted after 1936 by re-armament. Growing international tension meant increased defence spending.

The Problem of Mass Unemployment

This problem was the major social issue of the inter-war years. The 1930s acquired an evil reputation associated with images of the Dole queues, the hunger marches and the means test. From 1921, when the post-war boom began to falter, till 1940, Great Britain suffered mass unemployment on an unprecedented scale, with never less than one million people out of work. By the winter of 1920–1921, more than two million were unemployed. A modest recovery in the late 1920s was overtaken by a severe depression following the Wall Street Crash of 1929 and the world-wide decline in trade and industrial activity. Britain's worst years for unemployment were those after the financial and political crisis of 1931. In the winter of 1932–1933, unemployment reached its highest point with three million out of work. These did not include married women, farm labourers or the self-employed.

The level of unemployment depended on the cycle of boom and slump in world trade which affected Britain as a major trading nation. Thus the post-war boom was followed by a crash. A recovery in the mid and late 1920s was halted by the 1929 crisis, which shattered U.S. business confidence and reduced the level of world trade. The disruption of major economies such as the U.S. and Germany reduced their ability to trade with Britain. British exports in 1931–1932 were reduced to a half of what they had been in 1913.

Unemployment was worst in the staple export trades of shipbuilding, mining, steel and textiles. The Depressed areas were the regions where heavy industry was situated.

Unemployed as % of Insured Workers in the Regions

Region	1932	1937
London and the south-east	13·7	6·4
South-west	17·1	7·8
Midlands	20·1	7·2
North	27·1	13·8
Wales	36·5	22·3
Scotland	27·7	15·9
Northern Ireland	27·2	23·6

This structural unemployment in regions dependent on declining export industries was avoided in the south-east and the Midlands where much of the 'new' industry of the inter-war years was situated. As the 1930s wore on, the contrast between the reviving industries of the South of England and the depressed areas grew.

The 'Dole' and the Means Test

In 1911, a National Unemployment Insurance scheme was introduced. It was extended during and after the Great War to cover more workers. It ran into difficulties, as the numbers of unemployed rose in 1921–1922 and spells of unemployment increased. The scheme, originally intended to be self-supporting through contributions from the State, employers and employees, broke down as unemployment rose. Government contributions had to increase. The burden of financing unemployment benefit, costing the government £120 million per annum by 1931, only £44 million of which was met by contributions, played an important part in the political crisis which overthrew the Labour government of 1929–1931. In 1931, the National government introduced economy measures, reducing benefits by around 10%, withdrawing benefit from married women and limiting unemployment benefit to 26 weeks, after which a rigorous means test was applied. This involved visits to people's homes and detailed inquiries into their circumstances. On this basis, a new rate of relief was assessed. Many found that their relief was reduced or their benefit entirely taken away.

So the unemployed faced the complicated and often humiliating rules of unemployment relief. Although Britain's provisions were more generous than many other countries, including the U.S. which had no unemployment insurance till the 1930s, unemployment was a major cause of continuing poverty in Britain. 'Hunger marches' in the 1930s like the Jarrow Crusade in 1936 emphasized the plight of the unemployed.

29

The ideas of the economist J.M. Keynes that increased government spending without a balanced budget could increase economic activity were not widely accepted before the 1940s. In the inter-war years, the prevailing view was that a balanced budget and careful allocation of expenditure was essential to preserve business confidence and the value of the currency. The experience of mass unemployment between the wars was to convince much opinion of the need for more state intervention to improve social conditions.

The Collapse of the Labour Government in 1931 and the Formation of the National Government

The Labour government of 1929–1931 entered office just as the British economy was affected by the world depression. Labour followed 'orthodox' economic policies and the Chancellor, Philip Snowden, rejected any socialist measures. The problem of rising unemployment led the P.M., MacDonald, to seek the cooperation of the other parties.

When, in 1931, Britain faced a financial crisis and a collapse in foreign confidence in the £, the Labour Cabinet considered economies including cuts in unemployment benefit to restore foreign confidence in the currency. In the end the Cabinet split over the sacrifice demanded of the unemployed and resigned. MacDonald, to the amazement of the bulk of the Labour Party, agreed to head a National government which included Conservatives and Liberals.

The National government was in effect a disguised Conservative government (only 15 Labour M.Ps supported the National government). The Chancellor (Snowden) increased taxes and imposed economies, including reductions of wages for teachers, the armed forces, police and civil servants. Unemployment benefit was cut and a means test required for benefits beyond 26 weeks. In September 1931, there was a run on the £ after a mutiny of sailors at Invergordon. The men refused to accept a 10% wage cut. The government was forced to abandon the Gold Standard which made British goods cheaper abroad, as the £ soon stabilised at around two-thirds of its former value.

MacDonald was now a prisoner of the Conservative majority in his own government. It was the Conservatives who insisted on an election in October 1931. This ensured, in effect, nine more years of Conservative rule till 1940. The National government won a landslide majority of 497 seats, reducing Labour to only 46 M.Ps compared to 287 in 1929. The Liberals were split between supporters and opponents of the National government. The fact is that the Conservatives were the dominant party of the inter-war years: they were the main factor in the Coalitions of 1918 and 1931; the only elections of the period in which they failed to gain a majority of seats were in 1923 and 1929.

After the election in 1931, the National government abandoned Britain's traditional policy of free trade and imposed tariffs. The new Chancellor was Neville Chamberlain, who claimed it vindicated his father's work. (Joseph Chamberlain had campaigned in the 1906 election for tariff reform.) Duties on imports, excepting food and raw materials, varied between 10% and 33%, though Empire products were exempt. This increased the sales of British goods at home. Other countries were adopting protectionist measures at this time and the British government felt impelled to protect British markets so as to prevent further rises in unemployment.

Government assistance was given to industry and agriculture. To assist the farmer, imports were limited by quotas; marketing boards subsidised prices — the object being to raise prices for the farmer without raising them for the consumer. To help the ailing traditional industries, the government encouraged the reorganisation of shipbuilding, steel and coal mining. This was done by closing down obsolete factories and improving efficiency. In fact, the coal owners obstructed the work of the coal mines reorganisation commission. In the steel industry, an Iron and Steel Federation was formed in 1934 to reorganise and modernise plant. Similar reorganisation was done by the National Shipbuilders' Security Ltd.

In 1934, a Special Areas Act sought to improve employment prospects in the North, Scotland and South Wales, though its budget was inadequate. Attempts were made to encourage labour to transfer to the South where work was available, e.g. some Scottish steel workers moved to Corby in the Midlands. In 1934, the unemployment benefit cuts of 1931 were restored and income tax was lowered which added to consumer spending.

Slowly the economy recovered, though the depressed areas remained miserable. Unemployment fell from nearly three million in January 1933 to 1·6 million by 1936. In 1937, production was 20% above the level of 1929. Exports and imports, however, remained sluggish because of the decline in world trade. Accordingly, depressed areas dependent on exports suffered. For those in work the standard of living recovered. There was a housing boom in the 1930s, mainly in the private sector which benefitted the construction industry. There was also a growth of the consumer industries with increased sales of radios, electric cookers, refrigerators, telephones,

31

furniture and motor cars. In addition, from 1937 the threat of war and consequent rearmament helped the depressed areas to recover. By 1939, unemployment had fallen to 1·3 million.

It is significant that the British Fascist movement began in the period of Distress in 1931–1932. It was led by a former Labour M.P., Oswald Mosley, who formed the British Union of Fascists. He proposed a programme of public works to combat the Depression. Yet British Fascism never caught on, perhaps because of the threat from Fascism abroad.

The scale of the Depression meant that after World War 2, governments followed Keynesian policies of public spending and full employment which had been advocated but not accepted during the Depression. Labour's victory in 1945 was in many ways a reaction to memories of the Depression. More immediately, however, the Labour Party was again defeated in the Election of 1935. Baldwin's National government could point to a record of economic recovery, while there was, as yet, no confidence in a Labour government.

Essay Questions to Consider

1. "Too little, too late." Is this an adequate description of the National government's attempts to address the social and economic problems of Britain in the 1930s?

2. "Its economic policies contributed little to economic recovery." How accurate is this judgement on the National government of 1931–1940?

3. Discuss the political and economic significance of the formation of the National government in 1931.

4. What problems faced the National government in 1931 and how successful was it in dealing with them?

5. "We should praise the National Government (1931–1940) for doing so much for the economy and the unemployed, not blame it for failing to do more." Do you agree?

6. How true is the claim that the period between 1931 and 1939 was one of hardship for most British people?

7. Would you agree that "to concentrate on the Dole queues and the hunger marches" of the 1930s is to present a false picture of the decade?

8. Why was there mass unemployment in Britain between the two world wars?

5. THE POST-WAR LABOUR GOVERNMENT AND THE ESTABLISHMENT OF THE WELFARE STATE

1. The Beveridge Report

This Report, published during war time in 1942 by Churchill's Coalition government, was a landmark in the history of social security. Beveridge had been deeply involved with the problems of social security ever since, as a civil servant, he had worked with Liberal governments before 1914. He now produced a detailed scheme of comprehensive social insurance.

It built on the piecemeal provision of pensions, unemployment and sickness benefit, which had come into existence since 1908. The Plan proposed the total abandonment of the Poor Law mentality which had caused all payments to the old, sick and unemployed to be regarded as charitable offerings, to be kept as low as possible so as to deter idleness and extravagance. Beveridge insisted the plan was one of insurance — giving benefits of right in return for contributions. It was also assumed that there should be non-contributory children's allowances for each child after the first, paid for out of taxation and not out of insurance contributions. There was to be, in addition, a National Health Service to give everyone whatever medical treatment was required. Moreover, there should be an end to the mass unemployment that had plagued Britain in the 1930s.

This Report reflected the mood of Britain in the latter years of the war. Beveridge outlined what many felt they were fighting for. The Report became a best-seller. The unenthusiastic reception of the Report by P.M. Churchill helps to explain the Labour victory in the 1945 election, despite Churchill's heroic leadership of the war effort.

2. The General Election of 1945

In May 1945, the Labour Party withdrew from the war-time Coalition government headed by Churchill. The ensuing election in July was the first since 1935. The result was the first Labour parliamentary majority, Labour winning 393 seats to the Conservatives' 213 and the Liberals' 12.

This Labour victory was a reaction to the years of Conservative dominance, years associated with slump and unemployment. The Conservative campaign was negative, with Churchill launching ill-considered attacks on his former colleagues, including the suggestion that

33

a Labour victory would bring with it the threat of a native Gestapo. Although Churchill himself retained great prestige, his party lacked voter appeal. By contrast, Labour had a positive image with its manifesto, 'Let us Face the Future', calling for a sweeping programme of social reconstruction. Many felt that Labour was more sincere in its intentions to implement the war-time Beveridge Report.

The Labour leadership was confident and talented. As P.M., Clement Attlee proved a good chairman of the Cabinet which included Aneurin Bevan as Minister of Health, Hugh Dalton as Chancellor, Ernest Bevin as Foreign Secretary and Herbert Morrison as Home Secretary.

3.   Labour and the Creation of the Welfare State

All three parties in 1945 favoured extensive welfare provision but it fell to Labour to introduce the modern Welfare State. The Beveridge Report of 1942 wrote of the need for the state to attack the 'five giants of Want, Disease, Ignorance, Squalor and Idleness'. The Welfare State therefore envisaged the provision of comprehensive social services 'from the cradle to the grave', through a system of education, health, housing and social security.

The Labour government did not create the Welfare State out of nothing. Its origins must be sought in the Liberal government legislation of 1906–1914 which introduced Old Age Pensions and health and unemployment insurance. In the 1920s and 1930s, state action in the realm of social assistance was expanded; for example, the building of council houses and the extension of unemployment insurance and of old age pensions to cover more people. What was lacking however was a **comprehensive** provision of Welfare. The experience of the inter-war years confirmed much influential opinion in favour of more state intervention to improve social conditions.

4.   The Details of the Welfare Measures

(a) The Battle against Ignorance

The war-time Coalition government in 1944 passed the Education Act which the ensuing Labour government implemented. This raised the statutory school-leaving age from 14 to 15, and required all children to receive a secondary education without the payment of fees. The Act involved selecting children at 11 to determine whether a child would go to a grammar or a secondary modern school (in Scotland the rough equivalent was senior and junior secondary). In practice, the Secondary Modern schools were for the majority who failed the 11 plus examination. The eventual solution to this problem was to be the introduction of comprehensive schools but there was much opposition to the destruction of grammar schools entailed by the introduction of comprehensives. The main criticism of the 1944 Act was the inferior opportunities offered to children in Secondary Modern schools.

(b) *The Battle against Want*

Churchill's government also introduced the 1945 Family Allowance Act as an answer to family poverty. This provided for an allowance of five shillings a week for a second and each subsequent child. The amount was small and went to all, regardless of means, and was not therefore to be a long-term solution to the problem of family poverty.

The Labour government passed the National Insurance (Industrial Injuries) Act in 1946. Like the old Workmen's Compensation Acts, this provided for compensation for injury or disability resulting from accidents at work. However, whereas earlier legislation had made employers responsible for the payment of compensation, the new Act followed the Beveridge principle of compulsory and universal insurance for all employees against industrial injury, paid for by contributions from employers, employees and the state.

The main National Insurance Act of 1946 replaced the health, unemployment and pensions insurance schemes which had grown piecemeal since 1911 and substituted a comprehensive insurance scheme for sickness and unemployment benefit, retirement and widows' pensions and maternity grants. All adults of working age paid a weekly contribution which was supplemented by contributions from employers and the state. This provided for the first time a comprehensive basis for insurance provision.

In 1948, the remnants of the Poor Law were swept away, replaced by the National Assistance Act. This provided financial assistance for those outside the National Insurance scheme. National Assistance, though means-tested, was of benefit to many elderly people who did not have sufficient contributions to the National Insurance scheme.

(c) The Battle against Disease

The most striking welfare service was created in the National Health Service Act of 1946 which came into effect in 1948, under the superintendence of Aneurin Bevan, the Minister of Health. Building on the basis of Lloyd George's health insurance system of 1911, free medical care was provided, including dental and optical treatment and free prescriptions for everyone. Insurance contributions were far over-shadowed by subsidies from national taxation. The country's hospitals were nationalised and hospital care was provided without charge. In deference to the British Medical Association, the government did not abolish private medicine. Nevertheless, the N.H.S. contrasted with the situation before the war where those not insured had to pay for treatment. There were many problems with the new service, not least overcrowded and out-of-date hospitals and the cost of running the service. Indeed, in 1950, the government was forced to introduce charges for spectacles and dental treatment. Nevertheless, the N.H.S. won general acceptance as an essential aspect of a civilised society.

(d) The Battle against Squalor

Rehousing was an essential aspect of post-war reconstruction. However, economic conditions interfered with the housing programme and rehousing proceeded at a pace below national requirements. There was a lack of building workers and a scarcity of building materials. Bevan's target of building 200,000 houses a year was not met. Shortage of housing remained a problem for years to come. The Labour government restricted private house building in favour of council houses. The result was an inflation of costs and lengthy council house waiting lists.

Under the New Towns Act of 1946, fourteen New Towns were established under the Labour government, including East Kilbride and Glenrothes. They were intended to be well-planned and with sufficient employment to attract residents. In fact, though useful, the New Town programme did not greatly affect the location of industry or prevent an increase in the number of long-distance commuters.

(e) The Battle against Idleness

In 1944, a White Paper on Employment policy committed the government to the maintenance of a 'high and stable level of employment' after the war: there was to be no return to the mass unemployment of the inter-war years. And it did seem that the Labour government had done away with the pre-war evil of industrial depression. In contrast to the 1930s, Keynesian ideas of a managed economy and increased government spending without the need to balance the Budget were adopted. By 1946, unemployment was only 2·5%. That is not to say, however, that the economy was without its difficulties. Britain faced the burden of paying for increased social services and war debts and repairing war damage. The government tried to boost exports and extended rationing to control imports. American financial help was essential to get Britain back on its feet and in 1949 the £ had to be devalued, making exports cheaper and imports dearer.

Nationalisation

The 1945–1951 Labour government is associated not only with the welfare state but also with the nationalisation of basic industries. In 1946, the Bank of England was nationalised. The coal industry and civil aviation followed in 1947. In 1948, public transport, including the Railway network, was nationalised. So too were the electrical and gas industries. When iron and steel were taken into public control in 1949, this was opposed vigorously by the Conservatives, who denationalised the industry in 1953.

In the end, nationalisation was to prove an electoral liability to Labour. Other than in the coal industry, it did not much improve wages and working conditions in the industries involved; nor did it much improve the service to the public. It did not involve 'workers' control' or 'industrial democracy'. Most of Labour's nationalisation survived till the 1980s but there was little enthusiasm for carrying it further. The trouble was that nationalisation was applied on the whole to industries which were unprofitable and out-of-date or which required large injections of capital.

Conservative opposition to steel nationalisation led the government to introduce a new Parliament Bill in 1947 to amend the 1911 Parliament Act, so that the Lords' delaying power was reduced from two years to one year. The new Parliament Bill became law in 1949.

The End of the Labour Government

By 1950, it seemed as if the Labour government had run out of steam and in the election of that year, the government's majority was reduced to six. There was a yearning for an end to high taxation and rationing. In 1950, the Korean War plunged the economy into crisis: imports were made more expensive by the world-wide shortage of materials and the need for rearmament required economies in welfare spending. The Chancellor, Hugh Gaitskell, proposed charges for prescriptions which let to the resignation of Bevan, the Health Minister, and much dissatisfaction in Labour ranks. In the 1951 election, the Conservatives returned to power with a majority of 17. There was not to be another Labour government until 1964.

Essay Questions to Consider

1   "A document of far-reaching political and social consequences." How true is this of the Beveridge Report?

2.   "Britain should be praised for the significant advances made in education, housing and health between 1944 and 1951." Do you agree with this view?

3.   How true is it to say that the Labour Government of 1945–1951 set up the Welfare State?

4.   How successful were the welfare reforms of the Labour Government of 1945–1951 in improving social conditions in Britain?

5.   Account for the successes and failures of the Labour governments' domestic policies between 1945 and 1951.

6.   Account for the victory of the Labour Party in the 1945 General Election.

6. THE CHANGING POLITICAL IDENTITY OF SCOTLAND WITHIN THE U.K. IN THE PERIOD, 1850–1979, EXEMPLIFIED BY: ADMINISTRATIVE DEVOLUTION, NATIONALIST SENTIMENT AND THE DEVOLUTION DEBATE UP TO 1979

Definition of Terms

Scotland is a **nation**: most Scots feel themselves to be Scottish and share a common heritage. However Scotland is not a **state**; it is part of the U.K. state – since the 1707 Union of the Parliaments of Scotland and England, the U.K. has been a unitary state, with one Parliament and one Government.

Despite this however, Scotland has always enjoyed a considerable measure of **decentralisation**. Thus the Act of Union of 1707 recognised Scotland's distinctive institutions: the separate legal, religious, educational and local government systems. Scotland has a form of administrative devolution, i.e., the delegation of Central government powers to the Scottish Office in Edinburgh, with no loss of sovereignty, the ultimate power residing in the U.K. Parliament. Since the 19th century, there has been a persistent demand for **home rule** or **legislative devolution**, i.e., a Scottish Parliament **within** the U.K. This policy is to be distinguished from the demand for independence, where Scotland would become a nation-state, separate from England.

Administrative Devolution

There was a revival of Scottish Nationalism in the middle of the 19th century, as a reaction to the danger that Scotland was drifting into becoming merely 'North Britain'. There were complaints about the neglect of Scottish interests and in 1853 an Association for the Vindication of Scottish Rights was founded. Its meetings and petitions demanded that a Scottish Secretary should be restored to head a separate Scottish Administration, that Scotland should receive a larger share of Scottish representation at Westminster and a greater share of U.K. expenditure.

Governments at Westminster did respond to these complaints. Thus the second and third Reform Acts increased Scottish representation from 53 to 72 M.Ps. After a campaign led by the Liberal politician Lord Rosebery (1847–1929) for an overhaul in the machinery of government in Scotland, the Scottish Office was formed in 1885. This measure was passed by a Conservative government under Lord Salisbury. Until 1892, the Scottish Secretary was outside the Cabinet and his office was not in Edinburgh, but at

Dover House in Whitehall. Assuming the functions of the Home Office in Scotland, the Scottish Office gradually took over more and more responsibilities, including supervision of Scottish local government.

In 1926, the Conservative government upgraded the Scottish Secretary to a full Secretary of State. The transfer of functions to the Scottish Office continued and in 1939 the various Scottish departments were moved from Whitehall to St. Andrew's House in Edinburgh. The Scottish Office was now organised into four departments, namely Agriculture, Health, Education and the Home Department.

During World War 2, the Scottish Secretary in Churchill's Coalition Cabinet was Tom Johnston, the Labour M.P. for West Stirlingshire. He was a vigorous advocate of Scottish interests, securing a North of Scotland Hydro Electric Board in 1943. He promoted a separate Scottish Tourist Board and helped to create the Scottish Council on Industry, to establish links between government and industry. Johnston reminded his colleagues of the potential danger of a Nationalist movement in Scotland if Scottish interests were neglected.

Thus, prior to the introduction of the Scottish Parliament and Executive in 1999, the Scottish Office was a form of Administrative Devolution which, over the years, expanded greatly in scope. Its foundation in 1885 and its expansion thereafter were responses to periodic upsurges of Scottish Nationalism. The Scottish Office eventually had five departments:

1. Agriculture and Fisheries;
2. The Industry Department for Scotland;
3. The Home and Health Department, responsible for police, fire services, and the N.H.S. in Scotland;
4. The Scottish Office Education Department; and
5. The Scottish Development Department, responsible for housing, roads and local government.

The Scottish Secretary had four ministerial colleagues to assist him. Yet the breadth of a Scottish Secretary's responsibilities meant that he was often more involved in various aspects of government policy than many other Cabinet colleagues. It was a difficult balancing act to defend Scottish interests in the British government and at the same time represent the U.K government in Scotland, especially if the Scottish Secretary was of a different party from the Scottish parliamentary majority.

Legislative Devolution and Scottish Nationalism

In 1886, nationalist aspirations and the Irish example led to the formation of the Scottish Home Rule Association. Soon Liberal policy was one of 'Home Rule all round', i.e. Parliaments for Scotland and Wales as well as Ireland within the U.K. The Labour movement too supported Home Rule, though not the Conservatives or Unionists as they were called. On the eve of war in 1914, the Liberal government introduced a Scottish Home Rule Bill, only for it to be shelved with the outbreak of war. In Scotland, the home rule question never had the urgency or support which existed for Home Rule in Ireland. Liberal governments gave far greater attention to Irish Home Rule.

It was the failure to obtain a degree of self-government which led to the emergence of the Scottish National Party (S.N.P.). This was founded in 1934 as a result of a merger of the National Party of Scotland with the smaller Scottish Party. The S.N.P. made little impact. The Unionists were hostile as ever to Home Rule, while Labour gave the matter little attention.

In 1942, the S.N.P. split when its leading figure, John MacCormick, was defeated by a left-winger for the party chairmanship. MacCormick withdrew from the party and with his supporters formed the Scottish Convention. This seemed more effective than the S.N.P. In 1947, it called together a 'Scottish National Assembly' which demanded parliamentary devolution. In 1949, a National Covenant was drawn up proposing a Scottish Parliament though within the framework of the United Kingdom. The Covenant attracted nearly two million signatures but the two major parties were able to ignore the 'covenanters' because they were unable to influence voting preferences. Indeed the 1955 election gave the Unionists a majority of the Scottish constituencies, 36 out of 71.

The S.N.P. did win a by-election at Motherwell in 1945, when Dr. Robert MacIntyre became the first S.N.P. M.P. Yet the party did badly in elections, and it seemed that Scots did not want independence. Less than 1% of the electorate supported the S.N.P. during the 1950s. In the 1960s, the party's membership increased as did its support. This reflected a disillusion with the two major parties and concern at high levels of unemployment in Scotland. In 1967, Mrs. Winnie Ewing won a by-election for the S.N.P at Hamilton and since then, there has been a continuous S.N.P. presence in Parliament.

In the 1970 election, the S.N.P. lost Hamilton but won the Western Isles. In 1973, the S.N.P. won Glasgow Govan in a by-election. In the February 1974 election, the party lost Govan but held the Western Isles and won six other seats (four from the Conservatives and two from Labour). In the October 1974 election, the S.N.P. won eleven seats and took 30·4% of the Scottish vote.

Opinion polls suggested most Scots opposed independence but favoured Devolution. Discontent with Labour and Conservative governments helped the S.N.P. which in the 1970s adopted the slogan, "It's Scotland's Oil". The discovery of North Sea oil was of tremendous importance to the British economy at a time of rising oil prices, and the S.N.P. could claim that Scotland would benefit if it was under Scottish control.

S.N.P. gains led to concern at the possible break-up of the U.K. as the S.N.P. stood for independence. So Labour and Conservative considered schemes to devolve power to a Scottish Assembly controlling local affairs but with Scotland remaining a part of the U.K. Thus devolution was not S.N.P. policy but a response to S.N.P. electoral gains. Devolution became one of the main political issues of the 1970s.

In 1968, the Labour government set up a Royal Commission on the constitution which published its report in 1973 (the Kilbrandon Report). The matter became urgent with the S.N.P. gains in the 1974 elections and in 1976 the government drew up a bill to set up a Scottish Assembly.

This proposed a directly elected Assembly which would sit in Edinburgh with legislative powers over education, health, local government, agriculture and transport — mainly matters dealt with by the Scottish Office. In other matters such as overall economic policy, trade, defence and foreign policy, the U.K. Parliament retained control. The Assembly was to receive a block grant from Westminster.

The Labour government lacked a majority in the House of Commons and, against the government's wishes, a Devolution Bill was only passed in 1978, with the inclusion of a Referendum in which unless 40% of the Scottish electorate voted 'Yes' the Assembly would not be introduced.

The arguments in favour of Devolution were as follows.
1. The U.K. was over-centralised with too much political and economic power concentrated in the South of England.
2. Scotland as a nation with its own legal system must have more control over its own affairs.

Powerful arguments were, however, advanced against the proposals.

1. It would lead to arguments between the Assembly and Westminster, leading to the break-up of the U.K.

2. It would mean over-government, what with the recent creation of Regional and District Councils in Scotland.

3. It would devalue the role of Scottish M.Ps at Westminster and lead to a reduction in Scottish representation in the U.K. Parliament.

The referendum was held on 1st March, 1979. Of those who voted, 51·6% voted YES and 48·4% voted NO. Thirty-six per cent of the electorate did not vote at all. This meant that 33% of the electorate voted YES and 31% voted NO. Scotland did not get its Assembly because less than 40% of the Scottish electorate voted in favour. The S.N.P. regarded a majority of one as sufficient and their M.Ps took part in a No-Confidence motion along with the other Opposition parties which brought down the minority Labour government. In the ensuing election, the S.N.P. lost nine of their eleven seats and a Conservative government came to power opposed to legislative devolution.

Essay Questions to Consider

1. Explain the varying electoral fortunes of the Scottish National Party during the period 1945–1979.

2. "Support for Scottish nationalism has been primarily a response to economic hardship." How far do you agree with reference to the period 1930–1979?

3. How far did the political identity of Scotland change during the period 1850–1979?

4. Examine and account for the changes made at central government level to cater for Scottish affairs since 1885.

5. How far did Labour and Conservative governments bring administrative devolution to Scotland between 1945 and 1979?

6. How far did Scotland acquire a distinctive political identity during the period 1930–1979?

THE GROWTH OF NATIONALISM

INTRODUCTION

Reasons for the Growth of Nationalism in Europe in the Early 19th Century

Nationalism has been one of the most influential ideas of modern times. It has proved more enduring than Communist ideology, which sought to transcend national boundaries. The world has largely become organised on the basis of a system of states in which people claiming a similar nationality seek to control their own destinies.

To say what a nation is defies easy definition. Yet it is the case that most nationalities possess certain features which distinguish them from other nationalities. These include:

1. a common language;
2. shared customs and traditions;
3. similar religious loyalties;
4. a defined territorial area.

None of these factors is essential to the definition of a nation. What is essential is a state of mind inspiring the large majority of a people. It asserts that the nation-state is the ideal form of political organisation and the source of economic and cultural energy.

The Roots of Nationalism

Until the end of the 18th century, the word nation had only a legal and factual implication. A man's loyalty tended to be given not to the nation-state but to other forms of authority such as the city-state, a dynastic monarch, the Church or a feudal lord. In the 18th century, the aristocracy and the educated classes tended to be international and cosmopolitan in outlook. It is true that Latin was no longer the language of international discourse but it had been replaced by French as the accepted means of communication. Territories were exchanged by conquest or inheritance with little reference to the preference of their inhabitants. Thus Poland was partitioned in the 18th century between Austria, Prussia and Russia.

It was in the 19th century that the primary loyalty was given to the nation. The French Revolution of 1789–1799 and the subsequent Napoleonic Empire were of great importance in fostering this development. In France the nation came to embrace, not the aristocracy, but the people as a whole.

When Louis XVI escaped from confinement, the cry went up, "The King has escaped but the nation remains." A comprehensive system of national education was established to raise a new generation of patriotic citizens. The wars of the French Republic applied to a degree unknown before the national devotion and unity of the people.

Nationalism was also a reaction to the exactions and domination of the Napoleonic Empire, e.g. the Russian "Great Patriotic War" of 1812 against the invading French forces and the German "War of Liberation" of 1813 which led to the defeat of the French. In Italy and Germany, Napoleon indirectly supported the rise of nationalism by abolishing many feudal barriers in the way of greater national unity, e.g. in Italy he greatly reduced the number of states; in 1806 in Germany, he destroyed the antiquated Holy Roman Empire.

In the first half of the 19th century, the Romantic Movement assisted the growth of nationalist ideas. In literature, music and art, national traditions were extolled. Many nationalities showed a new interest in their own history and drew from it a new pride. Scholars and poets concentrated in writing in the vernacular language and in compiling dictionaries in their native tongues. National anthems were composed to arouse patriotism.

Nationalism threatened established Empires, in particular the Ottoman (Turkish) Empire and the Habsburg (Austrian) Empire. The Turks had conquered the peoples of the Balkans after the 15th century. In the 19th century, these peoples — Greeks, Serbs, Bulgarians and Roumanians — desired their independence. Hatred of the Moslem Turks and a veneration for a glorious past inspired the Greek revolt of the 1820s. The Greek Declaration of Independence began, "We, descendants of the wise and noble peoples of Hellas, we who are the contemporaries of the enlightened and civilised nations of Europe . . . find it no longer possible to suffer without cowardice and self-contempt the cruel yoke of Ottoman power which has weighed down upon us for more than four centuries." As a result of the Greek War of Independence, Greece became an independent Monarchy, though many Greeks remained under Turkish rule till the Balkan Wars of 1912–1913.

The Habsburg Empire too was threatened by the rise of nationalism. In 1815, after the defeat of Napoleon, the Congress of Vienna redrew the map of Europe. National feeling, as yet in its infancy, was largely ignored. Instead, the victorious powers tried to construct a system of states which would prevent French domination of Europe by re-establishing a Balance of Power.

The Habsburg Empire was intended to be a component part of the European balance. Yet it was the antithesis of nationalism. It was made up of many different peoples, united only by the ruling Habsburg Dynasty. The Empire consisted of Germans, Hungarians, Italians, Roumanians and Slav peoples such as the Czechs, Slovaks, Croats and Slovenes. Thus Austria was threatened with disintegration by the forces of nationalism. Before 1848, the various nationalities became increasingly discontented. The Austrian Chancellor, Prince Metternich, was cosmopolitan in outlook and refrained from having national sentiments. He opposed the Greek revolt as a dangerous precedent for similar unrest in Austria. In 1824, he remarked "I have for a long time regarded Europe as my Fatherland". The Habsburgs were able to survive the Revolutions of 1848 by playing on the rivalries of the different nationalities in a strategy of "Divide and Rule".

Nationalism has produced varying historical judgements. In the 19th century and after the First World War, nationalism was often portrayed as a dignified force and the multi-national Habsburg and Ottoman Empires villified as oppressive. Mazzini was typical of the Romantic attitude. He founded an association called 'Young Europe' to inspire German and Polish national aspirations. He believed in the comradeship of all nationalist movements. Of his native Italy, he spoke glowingly. Thus in 1861 he wrote that "unity was and is the destiny of Italy. The civil primacy twice exercised by Italy — through the arms of the Caesars and the voice of the Popes — is destined to be held a third time by the people of Italy — the nation."

A less sympathetic view of nationalism was held by some Liberals in the second half of the 19th century and became more widespread after 1945. Thus, in 1862, Lord Acton wrote of nationalism as "a retrograde step in history". Looking back at the events of 1848, J.S. Mill complained that nationalism makes men indifferent to the rights and interests "of any portion of the human species save that which is called by the same name and speaks the same language as themselves". In the 20th century, nationalism was carried to excess, notably with the rise of Fascist movements and the extreme biological nationalism of the Nazis. After 1945, ideas of internationalism and cooperation were in vogue and in Europe the breaking down of national barriers and misunderstanding came to the fore.

1. THE EMERGENCE OF GERMANY AS A NATION STATE AND THE PROCESS OF UNIFICATION IN GERMANY

1. Germany in 1815

In 1815, Napoleon's drastic reorganisation of Germany, in which he had abolished many of the smaller of the German states, was allowed to stand. In place of the 'Holy Roman Empire' which Napoleon had dissolved, the 38 German states were now organised into a loose union known as the German Confederation.

2. Factors Preventing German Unity

(a) *The German Confederation* was not a state. Each German state had its own government, military forces and taxes. Each state sent delegates to the Diet of the Confederation which met at Frankfurt. The stated aim of the Confederation was to maintain the independence of all the separate German states. Therefore the Confederation was a hindrance to the cause of German unity. In 1819, the Diet passed the Carlsbad Decrees which aimed to suppress liberal and national agitation and in 1832 the Six Articles permitted Federal intervention in states threatened with constitutional demands.

(b) *The Austrian Emperor* was given the Presidency of the German Confederation. (Until 1806, the House of Habsburg had filled the position of Holy Roman Emperor.) Austrian leadership of the Confederation was another hindrance to German unity. The Austrian Empire was mainly non-German, since the Slavs, Italians and Hungarians outnumbered the German speaking Austrians. Metternich, the Austrian Chancellor, was the arch opponent of nationalism which he saw as a threat to the integrity of the Austrian Empire. Large parts of this Empire, namely Hungary and Lombardy-Venetia, were outside the borders of the Confederation.

(c) *Austro-Prussian Rivalry* was another factor preventing German unity. Prussia was the only other German state able to compete with Austria in terms of population, size and wealth. Prussia had become a Great Power in the 18th century, due to the ability of its Hohenzollern rulers and the efficiency of their army and administration. The Prussian landowners or Junkers were supporters of absolute monarchy and opposed liberal and national demands. Moreover large parts of Prussia — West and East Prussia and Posen with a large Polish population — were excluded from the Confederation because only that part of the Prussian Kingdom which had been in the Holy Roman Empire was allowed to enter the Confederation.

(d) *Lack of Religious Unity.* Germany was not a country where the majority held to one religion. The Reformation in the 16th century had divided Germany between Protestantism and Roman Catholicism. The Prussian Rhineland, Austria and the South German states were Catholic, while much of the North and East were Protestant.

3. Factors Promoting German Unity

(a) *The Zollverein.* Prussia took the lead in forming a Zollverein or Customs Union. First, in 1818, Prussia abolished customs duties between her own scattered territories to permit a freer flow of trade. Then she persuaded some other north German states to join a customs union in 1828. This was followed in 1834 by the adherence of the leading South German states, Bavaria and Wurttemberg, along with Central German states. Prussia dominated this Free Trade area which did not include the Austrian Empire. The Zollverein assisted the industrial development of Germany and encouraged Prussian leadership in Germany at the expense of Austria. By 1848, Prussia seemed the main economic power in Germany.

(b) *The Growth of Liberal and National Feeling in Germany before 1848.* At first German nationalism was a reaction to French domination. Napoleon's conquest of much of Germany was assisted by Germany's lack of political unity and her political fragmentation. German Nationalists called for an uprising to drive out the French. Before 1848, most German Nationalists were also Liberals and demanded representative government and a free press.

4. The German Revolutions of 1848–1849

(a) *Events in Prussia.* King Frederick William IV (1840–1861) was a firm believer in the Divine Right of Kings. He opposed popular sovereignty and written constitutions, clinging to feudal ideas of loyalty. In 1847, he summoned a United Diet to approve the raising of funds to finance a railway linking Berlin and East Prussia. When the Diet demanded a constitution in return for agreeing to the request for finance, the King dissolved it. However, in March 1848, street disturbances in Berlin forced Frederick William to announce elections to a national assembly for Prussia. In December of the same year, he published a constitution for Prussia which retained great powers for the Monarch, though it did concede a Parliament.

(b) The Frankfurt Parliament. In 1848, revolts meant the German rulers including the Austrian Emperor lost authority and German Liberals and Nationalists demanded an all-German Parliament. This was intended to replace the German Confederation. The Parliament or National Assembly duly met at Frankfurt and drafted a Constitution by March 1849. This provided for a German Empire headed by a hereditary 'Emperor of the Germans' and an elected Parliament. In April, the Parliament offered the Crown to Frederick William of Prussia, who rejected it on the grounds that he could only accept the Crown if it was offered by his brother monarchs. In private, he referred to it as 'the Crown of shame'.

(c) Reasons for the Failure of the Frankfurt Parliament.

1. Hostility of the German Rulers. Once the German princes, including the Habsburg Emperor, overcame the revolution, they recovered their confidence. They opposed a German Empire in which they would lose their power.

2. The Austrian Emperor refused to accept a Germany which excluded the non-German parts of his Empire like Hungary and Lombardy-Venetia. Having successfully overcame the revolutions in the Habsburg Empire by 1849, the Austrian government warned it would not accept any breach in the unity of the Habsburg lands.

3. The Frankfurt Assembly lacked its own army and when it quarrelled with the King of Denmark, who ruled the largely German-speaking Duchies of Schleswig-Holstein, it had to rely on the Prussian army to attack the Danes.

5. Postscript: The Erfurt Union and the Humiliation of Olmutz (1850)

Austro-Prussian rivalry continued despite the failure of the Frankfurt Parliament. Prussian ministers supported a 'Kleindeutsch' or 'little German' solution to the German problem, i.e. the exclusion of Austria. They proposed a Union of North German states under Prussian leadership and summoned delegates to Erfurt to form such a union. However the Austrian minister Schwarzenberg refused to surrender Austrian supremacy in Germany. He persuaded the federal Diet at Frankfurt to threaten sanctions against any state which tried to break away from the Confederation. Russian support for Austria ensured a Prussian climb-down at Olmutz in 1850.

6. German Unification (1850–1871)

(a) Otto von Bismarck (1815–1898), who became the architect of German unity, was a conservative opponent of the Frankfurt Parliament and of the 1848 Revolution. He was a strong supporter of Prussia and her institutions. Between 1851 and 1859, he was Prussia's representative in the Diet of the German Confederation. Here he came to the conclusion that Austria, supported by the smaller states, would block changes in the Confederation to Prussia's advantage. Bismarck wanted Prussia to harness the force of German nationalism to ensure Prussian leadership in Germany at the expense of the Habsburg Empire. He was determined that any German unity would be achieved under the control of the Prussian army and King. Between 1864 and 1871, he secured German unity on his own terms. It must be emphasized that Bismarck did not and could not lay down a blueprint for German unification — that is to be wise after the event; rather he exploited a series of favourable situations to isolate his opponents and increase Prussia's power. In the 1860s, Bismarck was the supreme realist and exploiter of events.

(b) *The Prussian Constitutional Conflict (1860–1866)*

Bismarck became Minister-President of Prussia in 1862, not as part of a plan to unite Germany, but because of an internal Prussian conflict between King William I and the Liberal majority in the Prussian Parliament.

The Prussian government sought to strengthen the army and reduce the importance of the Landwehr or home-guard. The Liberals rejected these proposals between 1860–1862 and Bismarck was called to high office to break the deadlock. He proceded to carry out the army reform without securing parliamentary approval for the increased expenditure involved. Bismarck did not want the King's power over military affairs to be subject to parliamentary control. This constitutional deadlock continued till 1866, when Bismarck's successful foreign policy persuaded the Liberals to give approval to the extra-parliamentary collection of taxes. This was a decisive triumph for German Nationalism at the expense of Liberal parliamentary government.

(c) The Schleswig-Holstein Question (1863–1865)

This dispute was not of Bismarck's making. Since 1848, there had been a clash between the rival forces of Danish and German nationalism, both seeking control of the Duchies of Schleswig and Holstein. German nationalist opinion favoured the claims of the Duke of Augustenburg against that of the King of Denmark. In 1863, the new Danish King, Christian IX, precipitated a crisis by attempting to incorporate Schleswig into Denmark. This was contrary to the Treaty of London (1852) which provided that Denmark respect the autonomy of the two Duchies.

Bismarck had no intention of supporting the claims of Augustenburg; he wanted to acquire the Duchies for Prussia and thereby assert Prussian leadership in Germany. He knew there was little chance that the non-German Powers, Britain, France and Russia, would intervene in the crisis. To avoid unilateral Prussian action, Austria agreed to a joint Austro-Prussian invasion of the Duchies. After a short war, Denmark was forced to cede the Duchies to Austria and Prussia. (Treaty of Vienna, 1864.)

(d) The Austro-Prussian War of 1866

This was precipitated by the Schleswig-Holstein problem. In 1865, Bismarck secured a temporary settlement whereby Austria was to administer Holstein and Prussia would do likewise for Schleswig (the Convention of Gastein, 1865). In April 1866, Bismarck obtained an alliance with Italy for a war with Austria within three months, in which Italy would acquire Venetia as a reward. Bismarck was confident that Austria was isolated and that neither Russia nor France would intervene on her behalf. He now unleashed war on Austria by accusing her of not running Holstein properly. In June, Prussian forces occupied Holstein and attacked Austria and most of the other German states, following a Federal mobilisation against Prussia. The Prussian army, organised by Moltke, decisively defeated the Austrian forces at Sadowa in Bohemia (July 1866).

The Treaty of Prague (August 1866) signalled the end of the German Confederation whose formal abolition was declared. Prussia annexed not only Schleswig-Holstein, but also Hanover, Hesse-Cassel, Nassau and Frankfurt. All the remaining German states north of the river Main were to be incorporated in a new North German Confederation, ending permanently Austria's position in Germany. The North German Confederation was dominated by Prussia, which had five sixths of the population of the 23 states which were members. However, Bismarck did not desire the destruction of the Habsburg Monarchy. What he desired was the exclusion of the Austrian Empire from Germany.

(e) The Franco-Prussian War and the Creation of the German Empire (1870–1871)

A united Germany was forged as a result of the conflict with France. Bismarck did not plan the Franco-Prussian war. He was aware of the possibility of conflict following Prussia's overwhelming victory over Austria in 1866. The French Emperor, Napoleon III, demanded 'compensation' for Prussia's expansion in North Germany. He tried to purchase the Grand Duchy of Luxembourg from its ruler, the King of The Netherlands, but this produced an outcry from German nationalist opinion as Luxembourg had been a member of the German Confederation. The South German states, especially Baden, Bavaria and Wurttemberg, became alarmed at French ambitions and became ever more dependent on Prussia.

Bismarck was aware of French isolation: Italy resented the French garrison in Rome as an obstacle to complete Italian unity; Austria was in no position to fight Prussia; Russia was unsympathetic to Napoleon. In this favourable situation, Bismarck encouraged the cause of a Hohenzollern candidate for the vacant throne of Spain. When news of this leaked out, the French government reacted with fury and the candidature was withdrawn. What led to war was the French insistence that the project would never be renewed. Bismarck siezed an opportunity, by releasing to the press an edited version of the telegram he had received from King William. This reported the King's conversation with the French Ambassador in such a way as to convey the impression of an exchange of insults. France declared war and so caused the South German states, which feared French aggression, to support Prussia and the North German Confederation.

After the defeat of Napoleon's forces in Alsace-Lorraine, Bismarck negotiated with the four South German states for the creation of a German Empire under King William of Prussia.

Thus Bismarck had been remarkably successful in seizing his opportunities since 1862 to enable Prussia to dominate Germany and exclude Austria from German affairs. Victory in the Franco-Prussian War clinched the unification of the South German states with the North German Confederation. Germany had been created by military force and Bismarck had ensured the preservation of the power of the Prussian Monarchy.

(f) *The Prussian Army and Economy*

In addition to Bismarck's successful diplomacy, the unification of Germany was achieved by the Prussian army and was made possible by the strength of the Prussian economy. The Prussian army reforms were the work of Helmut von Moltke, who became Chief of Staff in 1857. He supervised a series of reforms increasing the size of the Prussian army and adapting modern transport and industrial methods to military needs. Prussia's railways were used for the swift transit of troops while the infantry were equipped with modern rifles and the artillery with effective guns.

Prussia's economy made it predominant in Germany. The acquisition of the Rhineland in 1814–1815 brought with it rich deposits of coal and iron. In the 1850s and 1860s, railway construction increased; an efficient banking system was created, while the steel industry thrived on government orders for modern artillery. Thus it can be said that the German Empire was founded not on 'blood and iron' but on coal and iron.

Essay Questions to Consider

1. Account for the growth of nationalism in Germany between 1815 and 1850.

2. How would you explain the lack of success of the nationalist movement in Germany in the period 1815–1860?

3 Why was there such a growth of national feeling in Germany during the period 1815–1870?

4. "Without the decline of Austria, unification would have been virtually impossible to achieve." How far do you agree in relation to Germany?

5. Account for the contribution of Bismarck in Germany to national unification.

6. Was Bismarck's success in unifying Germany between 1862 and 1870 due chiefly to the errors of others?

7. "Supreme opportunism was the key to unification." How far would you agree with this statement in relation to Bismarck and Germany?

8. "The role of political leaders in bringing about unification has been greatly exaggerated." Discuss this statement with reference to Bismarck in Germany.

9. How far would you agree that the growth of nationalism was caused by Austrian imperialism? Refer to Germany in the period 1815–1860.

10. Compare the influence of nationalism, economic factors and political leadership in the achievement of German unification.

2(a). A STUDY OF THE POLITICAL CHARACTER OF THE NEW NATION STATE IN GERMANY, WITH PARTICULAR REFERENCE TO THE EXERCISE OF ITS AUTHORITY

1. Germany under Bismarck 1871–1890

(a) The Constitutional Structure of Imperial Germany

In many respects the German Empire was an enlarged Prussia. Prussia made up over 60% of the Reich's area and its population. The German Emperor was also King of Prussia and the Chancellor was also the Prussian Prime Minister. The Emperor appointed and dismissed all Imperial officials from the Chancellor down. He was supreme commander-in-chief. The army swore allegiance to him, not to the constitution. Prussia had 17 votes in the upper House of Parliament, the Bundesrat, where amendments to the constitution could be defeated by 14 votes.

It is true there was a Reichstag elected by manhood suffrage but the Chancellor was not responsible to it for his actions. Its deputies never became ministers. It had only limited control over the Budget as it became the practice to approve the military budget for seven years. Bismarck was opposed to the parliamentary system of government such as existed in contemporary Britain or France.

(b) The Political Parties in Imperial Germany

The parties in the Reichstag could criticise but could not easily put their policies into practice. They were really pressure groups representing sectional interests rather than organisations for winning power.

The main parties were:
1. the Conservatives, supported by the Prussian landowners;
2. the National Liberals were admirers of Bismarck's achievements and had mainly middle-class support;
3. the Progressives were more radical, they opposed the militarism and authoritarianism of the German Empire, favouring genuine parliamentary government;
4. the Centre Party defended the interests of the Catholic Church and was strong in Bavaria and the Rhineland;
5. the Social Democrats represented the urban workers and were eventually to become Europe's most organised socialist party.

55

(c) Bismarck and the Kulturkampf

The years 1871–1878 are known as the 'Liberal Era' because Bismarck cooperated with the National Liberals, the dominant party in the Reichstag. They were strong supporters of national unity and measures were introduced to establish a national currency, set up a Reichsbank and achieve uniform legal procedures.

The National Liberals also supported the anti-clerical measures in the Kulturkampf or 'struggle for civilisation' between the Catholic Church and Bismarck. In the 1870s, there was a legal assault on Germany's Catholic minority. This was the product of Bismarck's dislike of the Centre party and liberal hostility to Papal Infallibility, proclaimed in 1870, which seemed to undermine the loyalty of Catholics to the new state. Bismarck also feared an alliance of Catholic France and Austria against the German Empire. The result was a series of anti-Catholic measures which restricted the authority of bishops and dissolved religious orders.

(d) Bismarck's Change of Course 1878–1879

In 1878, Bismarck ended his cooperation with the National Liberals. The years 1878–1879 saw several major changes in domestic policy.

1. Bismarck supported the introduction of tariffs which were sought by Prussian landowners and the iron and steel industry as protection against foreign competition. Many National Liberals were Free Trade supporters and disliked tariffs. There was also resentment that Bismarck would give them only a few ministerial appointments.

2. Bismarck abandoned the anti-Catholic campaign partly because anti-clerical measures in France ended any chance of a Catholic coalition against Germany. He also saw that the Centre party was only being strengthened by his attacks. The election of a new Pope in 1878 made compromise easier and in 1879 Bismarck secured the support of the Centre Party for his tariff proposals.

3. Bismarck desired to combat a new 'menace', that of Socialism within Germany.

(e) Bismarck and German Socialism

The introduction of universal suffrage in the German Empire in 1871 enabled the Socialists as the spokesmen of the urban workers to become a serious force in Germany. The increase in support for those influenced by Marxist ideas alarmed the Government. In 1878, Bismarck used two assassination attempts on the Emperor to obtain anti-socialist legislation. This remained in force until 1890 and was an attempt to destroy the organisation and the publications of the Social Democrats.

Bismarck also supported the introduction of comprehensive social security measures, in an attempt to undermine socialist support. This gave Germany the most comprehensive system of social insurance anywhere, against sickness, old age and accidents at work.

(f) The Fall of Bismarck

Bismarck failed to arrest support for the Socialists, who polled 20% of the vote in the 1890 Reichstag elections. In the same year, he resigned when William II opposed a renewal of the anti-socialist legislation. Bismarck, as Chancellor, remained dependent on the goodwill of the Emperor. In 1888, the new Kaiser, Wilhelm II, resented the position of the 'Iron Chancellor' and wanted to exercise power himself. Finally, he demanded Bismarck's resignation, so ending a career as chief minister which had begun in 1862.

(g) The Legacy of Bismarck's Domestic Policies

Bismarck succeeded in preventing Parliamentary Government and in preserving the power of the Prussian Monarchy — hence the relative weakness of the Reichstag and the political parties and the strength of the army and bureaucracy. Bismarck's political survival gave rise to the legend of Bismarck's infallibility. Yet after 1871 he was much less successful. He had always been dependent on circumstances and, after 1871, conditions were less favourable for the kind of triumphs he had enjoyed before 1871. He failed to develop a workable system of responsible government by concentrating excessive power in himself and the Emperor. He failed to provide an adequate successor to himself and power now passed into the hands of a young and headstrong Kaiser.

2. Germany Under Wilhelm II (1888–1918)

(a) The Chancellors after Bismarck

After the fall of Bismarck, there was an absence of central direction in the affairs of Germany. It was the Emperor, not the Chancellors, who set the tone of the age. William's interference and the calibre of the men selected to hold the post of Chancellor reduced the significance of the chief minister.

Caprivi (1890–1894), though a Prussian army officer, sought compromise and allowed the anti-socialist laws to lapse. His successors lacked his independence. Hohenlohe (1894–1900) became Chancellor when he was 75 years of age and was unable to restrain William's interference in policy. His successors, Bulow (1900–1909) and Bethmann-Hollweg (1909–1917), showed no exceptional ability.

(b) The Emperor Himself

William II was unstable and tactless. His inner insecurity resulted in a tendency to make snap decisions and irresponsible judgements. The Reichstag remained essentially an arena for criticism rather than responsible government. A vacuum of power led to the increased influence of the Army, of industrial combines and of nationalist pressure groups such as the Pan-German and Navy Leagues.

(c) Internal Conflicts

Down to 1918, the Prussian Parliament retained the undemocratic voting system introduced in 1849. This three-class system divided the electorate into three classes, according to the amount paid in direct taxes. Each class had an equal say in voting, though the first two classes, who paid the most, were numerically much smaller than class three. This reflects the persistence of powerful anti-democratic forces in Germany, despite the rapid social and economic changes in the late 19th and early 20th centuries.

In 1912, about one third of the electorate voted for the Socialists, who became the largest party in the Reichstag with 110 Deputies. The Centre Party also won sizeable representation with 91 Deputies. Yet due to the weakness of the Reichstag and the failure of the parties to work together, the Imperial system of government was unaltered. Increasingly, Germany's unresolved internal problems led to foreign policy adventures which distracted attention from domestic disputes.

The army held enormous influence because of the lack of firm control from the Kaiser and his ministers and the Reichstag's limited power over the military budget. In 1913, following high-handed action against civilians by some army officers in Zabern, Alsace (where the population resented German rule), the Reichstag passed a motion of no-confidence on Bethmann over his handling of the affair. Significantly, the government did not resign. Germany faced deadlock between the forces of conservatism and the supporters of a more modern political system.

(d) Economic Growth

The German Empire displayed a remarkable economic dynamism. Spurred on by political unification and the annexation of Alsace-Lorraine with its textile industry and iron-ore deposits, Germany became a rich and mighty power. The introduction of tariffs in 1879 protected industry from foreign competition, while the rise in population from 41 million in 1871 to 67 million in 1913 provided an expanding market. Later industrialisation than Britain meant Germany had the most modern plant.

After 1890, the industrial boom accelerated and by 1914, Germany had the greatest chemical, electrical and steel industries in Europe. By 1913, Germany produced 279 million tons of coal compared to 292 million tons in Britain, while Germany overtook Britain in steel output, producing over 13 million tons by 1910. The growth of shipbuilding and the manufacture of armaments were aspects of the growth of the iron and steel industries. In 1913, Germany's share of world trade was almost equal to that of Britain.

Two important features of German industrialisation were the growth of Kartells which were monopolistic industrial combinations able to control prices and the close relation of industry with Germany's banks which provided essential credit.

Essay Questions to Consider

1. "A country united in name only." How far would you agree with this judgement on Germany during the period 1871–1914?

2. How successful was Germany in dealing with internal political problems between 1871 and 1914?

3. How accurate is it to describe Germany as a united country after 1871?

4. How successfully did the constitutional monarchy in Germany win political support in the period 1871–1914?

5. "A period of prolonged crisis." Is this an accurate assessment of the years 1871–1914 in Germany?

6. "After 1871, Bismarck's domestic policies had the result of dividing rather than unifying Germany." Discuss.

7. Examine the causes and degree of political tension in Germany during the period 1890–1914.

2(b). THE IMPACT OF NATIONALISM ON THE INTERNATIONAL RELATIONS OF THE NEW STATE, 1871–1914

1. Bismarck's Diplomacy 1871–1890

(a) Aims

1. Bismarck accepted that Germany was a 'satiated' state, without territorial ambitions.

2. He sought to ensure the isolation of France, resentful at the loss of Alsace-Lorraine, imposed as a result of her defeat in the Franco-Prussian War.

3. He tried to keep both Austria-Hungary and Russia within the German orbit and avoid a conflict between them over influence in south-east Europe.

(b) Alliances

1. *The Three Emperor's League or Dreikaiserbund of 1872* was an informal agreement by the Emperors of Austria, Russia and Germany to keep the peace. In 1881, this became a formal treaty in which the three Empires agreed that if one of them was at war with a fourth Power, the other two would observe a benevolent neutrality. Though renewed in 1884, it lapsed in 1887 due to Austro-Russian antagonism over influence in the Balkans.

2. *The Dual Alliance of 1879.* Bismarck grew alarmed at Austro-Russian tension following Russia's attack on the Turks in 1877 in favour of the Slavs of the Balkans. Bismarck tried to avoid choosing between Russia and Austria by acting as 'honest broker' at the Congress of Berlin, 1878. However, Russia was angry at being forced to give up her hopes of dominating the Balkans. Accordingly, Bismarck sought closer relations with Austria and signed the Dual Alliance with her in 1879. This committed both to aid each other in the event of a Russian attack. Bismarck intended to tie Austria to Germany and prevent her allying with France. He also intended to prevent Austria provoking Russia.

3. *The Triple Alliance of 1882*. This involved Italy's adherence to the Dual Alliance and reinforced French isolation. Italy was angered at the French occupation of Tunis and promised to come to Germany's assistance if she was attacked by France.

4. *The Secret Reinsurance Treaty of 1887* involved Russia and Germany promising neutrality if either were at war with a third Power. This did not apply if Germany attacked France or Russia attacked Austria. While not strictly incompatible with the Dual Alliance, this required Germany to decide in the event of an Austro-Russian clash which was the aggressor.

(c) Assessment of Bismarck's Diplomacy

Bismarck left office with France isolated through German links with Austria, Italy and Russia. As for Great Britain, her colonial quarrels with France and Russia avoided an Anglo-French agreement or an anti-German coalition. Yet even before Bismarck's fall, France and Russia were drawing together. Both disliked Great Britain, while Russia was increasingly reliant on French loans. Dislike of Austria and resentment of German power led Tsarist Russia into the arms of Republican France. Bismarck, therefore, was unable to prevent a deterioration in Russo-German relations. However, it must be remembered that Bismarck's foreign policy was one of limited aims. He was satisfied with Germany's place in the European Balance of Power and avoided the world-wide aims of William II.

2. German Foreign Policy under William II (1888–1914)

(a) The Franco-Russian Alliance

In 1890, the Reinsurance Treaty was not renewed and in 1892 France escaped from isolation by signing a military alliance with Russia. Russia was to go to war if France were attacked by Germany and France promised to come to Russia's help if she were attacked by Germany. From now on Europe was organised into two camps and Germany was no longer able to direct the affairs of Europe. The German General Staff soon drew up plans which assumed that in any future conflict, Germany would face a war on two Fronts (the Schlieffen Plan).

(b) Weltpolitik

After Bismarck's fall, William II launched on his 'New Course', seeking world leadership for Germany (Weltpolitik), rather than merely primacy on the Continent. The Kaiser sought a 'place in the sun' and a great navy for Germany. German policy thus became restless and ambitious. Pan-German feelings increased and German influence was extended to areas hitherto ignored, such as the Balkans and the Ottoman Empire.

(c) Naval Policy

William II favoured a large navy. His agent was Admiral von Tirpitz, State Secretary for Naval Affairs from 1897. Naval expansion began from the late 1890s, enabling the German navy to challenge British supremacy of the seas. This meant a deterioration in Germany's relations with Britain. Britain was the one major European Power with whom Germany had no potential Continental argument, and whose friendship might have offset the Franco-Russian Alliance. However, it was not to be and between 1906–1914 Britain and Germany indulged in a feverish 'Naval race'.

(d) German Fear of Encirclement

German policy aroused widespread apprehension, especially in Russia and Britain. It led to Germany's isolation and her fear of encirclement. Britain settled her quarrels with France and Russia. Germany's diplomatic weakness was illustrated by the Moroccan Crisis of 1905–1906. The Anglo-French Entente of 1904 had as one of its main points a British agreement to help France add Morocco to its North African Empire, in return for which France accepted British rule in Egypt. The Kaiser attempted to break Anglo-French friendship by visiting Tangier in 1905 and demanding an international conference to discuss Morocco's future. At first, this produced a German success: the resignation of the French Foreign Minister, Delcassé, the architect of the Anglo-French Entente and opponent of the German demand for an international conference to decide the status of Morocco. Yet, at the Algeciras Conference in 1906, only Austria-Hungary supported Germany in opposing French predominance in Morocco. This rebuff did much to confirm German fears that the jealousy of her neighbours was

63

leading them to pursue a deliberate policy of encirclement, aimed at stifling her natural growth.

In the Bosnian crisis of 1908, caused by Austria's annexation of Bosnia-Herzegovina, the German Chancellor, Bulow, gave the Austrians unequivocal support. Germany assured her ally that, if necessary, Germany would mobilise in support of Austria-Hungary. This forced Russia to reluctantly accept Austria's action.

Another Moroccan crisis in 1911 worsened relations between Britain and Germany and weakened the support in both countries for reductions in naval building programmes. A German gunboat, the *Panther*, was sent to Agadir, allegedly to protect German commercial interests threatened by French expansion in Morocco. This raised British fears over German naval activity. Although the Germans accepted a settlement of the Moroccan question with the French, the crisis confirmed British suspicions of the Germans.

(e) Germany and the Outbreak of the First World War

After Germany's defeat in 1918, the victorious allies blamed Germany for starting the war ('War Guilt'). In the 1920s, German scholars tried to show that all the powers and not merely Germany were responsible. This view became influential and even seemed to justify the appeasement of Hitler in the 1930s. However, in the 1960s, the German historian, Fritz Fischer, argued that Germany sought to establish a world power position and European hegemony.

In 1914, the German government was prepared to risk war to establish German predominance. The German Army, under General von Moltke, was alarmed at the encirclement of Germany, seen in the close relationship of France, Russia and Britain. It was argued that it would be better to fight before French or Russian military strength became too great for Germany. It was therefore imperative to strike while Germany was sure of winning.

Fischer also claims that German War Aims, formulated in September 1914, for annexation and expansion at the expense of France, Belgium and Russia, predate 1914 and the outbreak of war. These involved a 'Mitteleuropa' — a German-dominated Central Europe as well as a large German colonial Empire.

In the July crisis of 1914, involving Austria-Hungary and Serbia, German policy was to urge Austria to take whatever action was necessary to maintain Austria's position as a Great Power. Yet an Austro-Serbian War was likely to lead to a general European War, for Russia was close to Serbia. The German government was prepared to take this risk. The feeling of encirclement plus the internal problems of the German Empire, including the determination of the ruling circles to resist democratic reforms, tempted the political and army leaders to resort to a violent solution.

Essay Questions to Consider

1. How far did the need for self-preservation influence the international relations of Germany between 1871 and 1914?

2. To what extent did domestic political problems affect the foreign and imperial policy of Germany during the period 1871–1914?

3. "Brilliant in execution but destined to fail." Discuss this assessment of Bismarck's foreign policy after 1871.

4. Assess German responsibility for the outbreak of World War 1.

5. How successfully did German foreign policy between 1871 and 1914 promote German interests?

3. IN RELATION TO GERMANY, THE NATURE OF FASCISM AND THE REASONS FOR ITS VICTORY

The Weimar Republic, 1918–1933

It is convenient to study Germany from 1918–1933 in three periods.

(a) 1918–1923 saw near-successful attacks on the Republic from both the extreme Left and Right, hyper-inflation and serious disorder.

(b) 1923–1929 were years of apparent stability and prosperity.

(c) 1929–1933 saw rising unemployment and despair, a breakdown of order and the collapse of Parliamentary government.

(a) 1918–1923

1. The German Revolution of 1918–1919

   Germany underwent Revolution in 1918–1919; a product of war weariness and the collapse of Germany's military effort in World War 1. In October 1918, sailors in the North Sea fleet mutinied and soviets or councils of soldiers and workers spread throughout Germany. In November, Kaiser William II was forced to abdicate and a Republic was proclaimed.

   Although the socialists led by Frederich Ebert formed a government, they were forced to work with the Army High Command against the more extreme socialists who formed the Communist Party in December. In 1919, the Army crushed the 'Spartacist' Rising in Berlin, in which the Communist leaders Karl Liebknecht and Rosa Luxemburg were brutally murdered.

   This opened up a rift between the Socialists committed to parliamentary democracy and the Communists who supported a Bolshevik Revolution. The use of the army and the Free Corps (volunteer units raised by the army command) strengthened extreme nationalist elements. These maintained that the army had not been militarily defeated in 1918, but had been 'stabbed in the back' by socialists, Jews, pacifists and republicans. In April 1919, Federal forces crushed a 'soviet' which had been set up in Bavaria.

   The Revolution of 1918–1919 gave Germany a democratic Republic whose constitution was worked out by an elected National Assembly, meeting at Weimar. This made provision for a Reichstag elected by proportional representation, and a popularly elected President who chose the Chancellor to head the government which required the support of a majority of elected deputies.

However, the Revolution failed to alter the structure of German society. In particular, it aroused the opposition of the Nationalists because it was associated with the Treaty of Versailles, under which Germany lost territory, was required to pay reparations and was saddled with 'War Guilt'. The danger of Right-wing extremism was revealed early on by the Kapp Putsch of 1920, in which Free Corps units tried to seize power in Berlin. The army failed to protect the Republic and only a general strike led to the collapse of the Putsch. A series of assassinations of Republican leaders took place, including Matthias Erzberger (1921), the leader of the Armistice delegation and the Jewish Foreign Minister, Walter Rathenau (1922).

2. 1923 — Crisis Year for the Weimar Republic

In 1923, the French Prime Minister ordered the occupation of the industrial Ruhr after Germany was declared in default on its reparations payments. This aroused fury in Germany and a policy of 'passive resistance' (a general strike) was adopted to defeat the occupying French and Belgian forces. Germany's financial condition worsened under the impact of the occupation and the policy of printing more and more money to bridge the gap between government income and expenditure.

In August, Gustav Stresemann, leader of the German People's Party, became Chancellor. He was determined to defeat inflation and secure the withdrawal of the occupying forces from the Ruhr. He ended 'passive resistance' and issued a new currency, but faced opposition from the State government of Bavaria, where Right-wing forces opposed what they saw as a sell-out to the French. In addition, in central Germany and in Hamburg, Communists made what proved to be their last attempt to carry out revolution.

In Munich, Hitler, leader of the National Socialist German Workers' Party (N.S.D.A.P. or Nazi) won publicity by his Putsch in which he attempted to persuade the Bavarian authorities to support him in a challenge to the government in Berlin. In fact, the State police fired on the Nazi column and Hitler was imprisoned. The events of 1923 had a lasting impact: they destroyed the confidence of many middle class people whose incomes and savings were wiped out at a stroke.

(b) 1923–1929

These years saw the apparent success of the Weimar Republic in achieving stability. The main reasons for this were:

1. the new currency issued at the end of 1923. It helped to check the inflation and restore confidence in the value of money; and
2. the Dawes Plan of 1924, which provided for foreign, mainly American, loans to enable Germany to pay reparations. This secured the withdrawal of troops from the Ruhr in 1925 and the recovery of the economy.

Gustav Stresemann, though Chancellor only from August–November 1923, remained Foreign Minister till his death in 1929. He provided an element of stability in a rapid succession of governments. He secured the Locarno agreements with the Western Powers in 1925 for a mutual recognition of frontiers. While this involved an acceptance of the demilitarisation of the Rhineland, it prevented another unilateral French occupation of the Ruhr. In 1926, Stresemann secured Germany's entry to the League of Nations. In the 1928 elections, the Socialists won their best result since 1919 with 153 deputies, while the Nationalists, Nazis and Communists had a poor result. In 1929, Stresemann obtained further concessions from the Allies, namely the Young Plan, for a further reduction in German reparation payments and the evacuation of Allied forces from the Rhineland ahead of schedule.

(c) 1929 – 1933

The Weimar Republic was undermined by the international economic crisis in 1929, which ended foreign loans, increased bankruptcies and unemployment which reached six million by 1932–1933. The last three Chancellors before Hitler — Bruning 1930–1932, Papen 1932 and Schleicher 1932–1933 — ruled without a parliamentary majority, being dependent on emergency decrees, issued under Article 48 of the constitution, which empowered the President to rule by decree if public order was threatened. Increased support for the Nazis and the Communists, as well as the collapse of the middle-class Liberal parties, undermined parliamentary government. In 1930, the Nazis became the second largest party in the Reichstag. The army and Conservative circles intrigued with President Hindenburg to introduce an authoritarian regime. In vain did Papen try to get the support of the Nazis, whose S.A. attacked Socialists, Communists and other opponents on the streets. In July 1932, the Nazis became the largest single party. Although, in November 1932, they lost two million votes, they remained the largest single party. Hitler was appointed Chancellor by Hindenburg in January 1933. He led a coalition of Nationalists and Nazis, and it was mistakenly believed that the Nazi movement could more easily be controlled if Hitler was given the responsibility of power.

(d) Explanations for Rise of Hitler

1. The Weimar Republic was associated with the defeat of 1918 and was saddled with responsibility for the Treaty of Versailles.

2. The proliferation of parties made decisive government difficult. There were at least seven sizeable political parties — K.P.D. (Communists), S.P.D. (Socialists), the Catholic Centre party, the Liberal parties, namely D.D.P. (Democratic party) and D.V.P. (People's party), D.N.V.P. (Nationalists) and N.S.D.A.P. (National Socialists). The K.P.D. and N.S.D.A.P. were committed to the destruction of parliamentary government.

3. The division between Socialists and Communists arising from the events of 1919 explains the failure of the Left to resist the rise of the Nazis. The middle-class Liberal parties were also divided between D.D.P. and D.V.P., the former being more in favour of the Republic and the latter being less inclined to welcome the demise of the Empire.

4. The economic crises of 1923 and 1929 undermined the Weimar system. The inflation of 1923 and the unemployment after 1929 caused many Germans to turn to the extreme Left or Right.

5. Account must be taken of Hitler's extraordinary ability as an orator and his nationalist propaganda, which played on the refusal of the German people to accept the verdict of 1918. Hitler's personality, will-power and self-confidence are all important in the rise of Nazism. After the failure of his attempt to seize power in 1923, Hitler accepted the need to contest elections and to seek power by 'legal' means. Fear of Communism and the promise to end unemployment were important factors in attracting support. There was a strong feeling, especially among the young, that the Weimar 'system' had failed and that by contrast the Nazis offered a break with the past.

Essay Questions to Consider

1. Assess the importance of economic factors in the rise to power of the Nazi party in Germany between 1918 and 1933.

2. "The part played by the leader was decisive in the rise to power of Fascist parties." Discuss this judgement with reference to Germany between 1919 and 1933.

3. "Aggrieved nationalism together with economic distress made possible the triumph of National Socialism in Germany." Do you agree?

4. How important a factor was propaganda in aiding the Nazi party to come to power in 1933?

5. What factors explain the collapse of democracy in the Weimar republic?

6. How far was the achievement of power by Fascists in Germany due to the absence of strong central government?

7. "The economic depression of 1929–1932 was the turning point in Nazi fortunes." How well does this explain Hitler's achievement of power in 1933?

4. IN RELATION TO GERMANY, THE NATURE OF FASCIST AUTHORITY AND THE USE OF POWER TO 1939

Nazi Germany 1933–1939

(a) Nazi Doctrine

Throughout his life, Hitler emphasized the importance of race — the alien Jews; the Aryans who were the Master Race and of whom the Germans were the purest strain; the inferior Slavs of Eastern Europe where Lebensraum or living space must be won. Hitler also sought to replace parliamentary democracy, Liberalism and Marxism with a National Movement obedient to the Leader or Fuhrer. The Nazi movement was influenced by Italian Fascism with its bold seizure of power.

(b) Dictatorship Established

In 1933, a one-party state was established in Germany. The process of coordination or 'Gleichschaltung' is used to describe the transformation of Germany from a federal parliamentary state to a unitary dictatorship. Important in this process were the following:

1. The Reichstag elections of March 1933, held in an atmosphere of terror following the burning of the Reichstag building in February and the use of emergency powers against opponents of the Nazis. The N.S.D.A.P. won 43·9% of the vote. At this time the S.A. terrified opponents and the first concentration camps appeared.

2. The Enabling Law of March 1933 was passed by the necessary two thirds majority in the Reichstag, through the expulsion of the K.P.D. deputies and the support of the D.N.V.P. and the Centre. This suspended the constitution and gave Hitler the power to issue laws.

3. Nazi pressure on the federal states involved the imposition of Nazi governors in April. In 1934, the federal system was abolished: Germany became a centralised, unitary state for the first time.

4. In July 1933, all political parties outside N.S.D.A.P were abolished. Elections in November 1933 produced a Nazi-packed Reichstag.

5. A Ministry of Propaganda under Joseph Goebbels censored film, radio, the press and cultural activity. Education was purged of

71

politically unreliable teachers and Nazi ideas were introduced into the curriculum.

6. The Trade Unions were replaced by a pro-Nazi German Labour Front under Robert Ley. Strikes were made illegal. The civil service also lost its independence and was subject to Nazification.

(c) The Night of the Long Knives, 30th June 1934

The Brown-Shirts or S.A., led by Ernst Röhm, wanted to assume control of the German Army. This aroused alarm among army officers while the casual violence of the S.A. angered many Conservative interests. Hitler needed the army's support in his determination to succeed the ailing President Hindenburg and unite the offices of President and Chancellor. The price of that support was Röhm's removal. In any case, Hitler needed the army for his ambitious foreign policy. Accordingly he ordered the purge of the S.A. leaders, using the black-shirted S.S. under Himmler as the agents of death. He publicly justified the murders to the Reichstag. At the same time, many opponents of the regime, including the former Chancellor Schleicher, were conveniently killed. When, in August 1934, President Hindenburg died, Hitler assumed the title of Führer, combining in his own person the offices of Chancellor and President. The army now took a personal oath of loyalty to Hitler. The German army was, in effect, an instrument in Hitler's hands. In 1938, Hitler was able to summarily dismiss both the War Minister, General von Blomberg, and the Commander-in-Chief, General von Fritsch. Finally, the Purge of 1934 saw the rise of the S.S. to a position of complete control of the police system and the concentration camps. Whereas the S.A. was a mass organisation, the S.S. was an elite force under Hitler's control.

(d) Anti Semitism

Hitler's hatred of the Jews was pathological. The Jew was held responsible for the 'stab-in-the-back' in 1918, and for Bolshevism. The 'final solution' of the Jewish problem during the Second World War, when millions of European Jews were murdered, was fore-shadowed by the attacks on Germany's Jewish population before 1939. After the dismissal of Jewish officials and the boycott of Jewish businesses came the 'Nuremberg Laws' (1935) depriving Jews of citizenship and forbidding marriage between Jews and Aryans. In November 1938, in the 'Kristallnacht' or Crystal Night, Jewish property throughout Germany was looted and destroyed. In January 1939, Hitler ominously declared that a European war would mean the annihilation of the Jewish race in Europe.

(e) The Economy under the Nazis

Hitler had risen to power with the support of many German industrialists. He had become Chancellor in coalition with Conservative Nationalists. He benefitted from the widespread belief that he would combat Bolshevism. In office, he presided over the destruction of independent Trade Unions while unemployment, which had ruined the Weimar Republic, was reduced. This reflected an intensified public works programme. Unemployment fell from 6 million to 2.5 million within 18 months of the Nazi advent to power. The introduction of conscription in 1935 further helped the unemployment problem, as did the expansion of heavy industry to meet the needs of rearmament. By 1939, there was a labour shortage in Germany.

Essay Questions to Consider

1. "Fascist rule could only exist by exploiting the fears of the masses." To what extent would you agree with reference to Germany up to 1939?

2. "To maintain its authority, Fascism relied on propaganda rather than on solid achievement." How far do you agree, with reference to Germany up to 1939?

3. Assess the impact of Fascist rule on the people of Germany up to 1939.

4. Why did Hitler's domestic policies from 1933 to 1939 enjoy much popularity in Germany?

5. Examine the changes in German society in the 1930s.

6. How far did the Fascist state depend on fear rather than popular support for its survival? Discuss with reference to Germany 1933–1939.

7. "The regime, after all, gave most Germans what they wanted." How justified is this view of Nazi rule in Germany between 1933 and 1939?

5. THE EMERGENCE OF ITALY AS A NATION STATE AND THE PROCESS OF UNIFICATION IN ITALY

1. Italy in 1815

The Congress of Vienna was determined to prevent any further attempt by France at European domination. So it re-established the state-system in the Italian peninsula similar to that before the French intervention during the Revolutionary and Napoleonic periods. Thus there were seven sizeable states: Piedmont, Lombardy-Venetia, Tuscany, Parma, Modena, the Papal States and the Kingdom of Naples (including Sicily).

2. Obstacles to Italian Unity

(a) *The Austrian Empire* dominated the peninsula through direct rule of Lombardy and Venetia, by Habsburg or Austrian rulers of the three central Italian Duchies of Tuscany, Parma and Modena and by the intimidating presence of the Austrian army. Metternich, the Austrian Chancellor, was determined to ensure that Italy remained a 'geographical expression'. In 1820–1821, the Austrian army crushed liberal revolts in Naples and Piedmont and in 1831–1832 in Parma, Modena and the Romagna.

(b) *The restoration of the Pope* as a temporal sovereign of the Papal States which included not only Rome but also the Romagna and the marches on the east of the Apennines. During the French Revolution, the Pope had been carried off to France and Napoleon had ended the Papacy's temporal power. After 1815, the Roman Catholic Church won back much of its former prestige in the reaction against the French Revolution. The Pope was a universal figure as head of the world-wide Roman Catholic Church and was an obstacle to liberal and national aspirations in Italy.

(c) There was *a lack of national feeling*. Only a small number of Italians were educated and supporters of national unity. The peasant population, mainly illiterate, was largely apathetic and unmoved by Italian nationalism.

(d) There were strong *local loyalties*. The Italian rulers did not wish to lose their status; all were absolute and there were no representative assemblies. Italy even lacked a Confederation, as in Germany. Differences of dialect hindered communication between Italians. Customs barriers, not only between but within states, hampered trade.

3. **Advocates of Italian Unity**

   (a) *Guiseppe Mazzini (1805–1872)* devoted his life to the cause of Italian national unity. In 1831, he founded 'Young Italy', whose mission was one of education and propaganda. Mazzini's programme was revolutionary in that he advocated the popular overthrow of all the Italian rulers and the setting up of a unitary Republic. His views were influential and he drew attention to the national cause.

   (b) *Vincenzo Gioberti (1801–1852)* was a Piedmontese priest who in 1843 published *Of the Moral and Civil Primacy of the Italians*. In this important work he proposed an Italian federation under the Pope's presidency. Gioberti sought to harness the Church to Italy's national revival. Unlike Mazzini, he rejected revolutionary methods. When, in 1846, a seemingly liberal Pope — Pius IX (1846–1878) — was elected, it appeared that Gioberti's programme was being implemented.

   (c) *Charles Albert*, King of Piedmont (1831–1849), was also seen as a leader who might free Italy from foreign domination. Piedmont was ruled by an ambitious dynasty — the House of Savoy — which had traditionally sought to expand its domains. In the 18th century, it had acquired the island of Sardinia and in 1815 it added the territory of the former Republic of Genoa. In 1848, Charles Albert proclaimed "Italia fara da se" (Italy will manage by herself) and led his army into Austrian-ruled Lombardy. This was the first active assistance by an established ruler in aid of the National cause.

4. **1848–1849 and the First War of Italian Independence**

   (a) *Events of the Revolutionary years*

   In 1848, revolts in all the Italian states forced the rulers to grant representative assemblies and constitutions. For example, in Piedmont, Charles Albert accepted a constitution known as the 'Statuto', which introduced an elected parliament on a restricted franchise. The Austrians were expelled from Milan and Venice and the Austrian Empire was paralysed by revolutions throughout the Habsburg lands. In March, Charles Albert, supported by troops from other parts of Italy, went to war with Austria. However, General Radetsky, the Austrian commander, defeated Charles Albert's army in Lombardy at Custoza in July. Moreover, the Pope denounced the war against Austria. As Head of the Catholic Church, he could not condone a war between Catholics

These reverses 'radicalised' the revolution. Venice became a Republic and in 1849, a Roman Republic was set up with Mazzini as the leading figure. Charles Albert again declared war on Austria, though he was once more defeated at Novara in Piedmont and abdicated. Moreover, a French force overthrew the Roman Republic and Venice was bombarded into submission by the Austrians.

(b) Lessons of the failure of 1848–1849

1. Italian nationalists abandoned reliance on the Pope as an Italian leader.

2. Habsburg military victories demonstrated Italy's need for a foreign ally and the unrealistic policy of 'Italia fara da se', i.e. avoidance of foreign help.

3. Piedmont's important position in the Italian national cause was clear. She alone of the Italian states kept a constitution after the defeat of the revolution; her dynasty under Victor Emanuel II (1849–1878) remained independent of Austria; Piedmont had a free press and attracted exiles from other parts of Italy.

5. Italian Unification 1850–1870

(a) Count Camillo Cavour (1810–1861)

Cavour was Prime Minister of Piedmont from 1852 till his death in 1861 (save for a brief period in 1859–1860). He was liberal in outlook and a supporter of Piedmont's constitution but he was opposed to the revolutionary methods of Mazzini. In the 1850s, he achieved much in ensuring that Piedmont's economy was efficient, e.g. he reduced tariffs and encouraged the development of railways.

(b) The Plombières Agreement (1858)

Cavour knew that a French military intervention was essential for the liberation of North Italy from the Austrians. In 1858, at Plombières, he secured the agreement of the French Emperor, Napoleon III, for Piedmont to obtain Venetia and Lombardy after the defeat of the Austrians and for France to receive, by way of a reward, Nice and

Savoy from Piedmont. It was envisaged that the Pope and the Kingdom of Naples would be left undisturbed.

(c) The Second War of Italian Independence, 1859

In 1859, Austria dispatched an ultimatum requiring Piedmont to disarm. In the ensuing war, France and Piedmont defeated the Austrians at two battles, Magenta and Solferino, in Lombardy. Napoleon now concluded an armistice with the Austrian Emperor at Villafranca. This left Venetia in Austrian hands while securing Lombardy for Piedmont. Napoleon was concerned at Prussia's mobilisation in the Rhineland, which was a threat to France. He was also alarmed at events in the central Italian Duchies, whose rulers had fled following revolts which led to demands for union with Piedmont under the slogan, 'Italy and Victor Emanuel'.

Cavour resigned office after Villafranca, furious at the failure to secure Venetia. However, he returned to power in 1860 and secured France's acceptance of Piedmont's acquisition of the three Italian Duchies of Tuscany, Parma and Modena in return for the cession of Nice and Savoy to France. This completed the first stage in Italian unification.

(d) The Expedition of the Thousand and the Acquisition of Naples and Sicily

The next phase in Italian unification involved Guiseppe Garibaldi (1807–1882). Unlike Cavour, he had been a supporter of Mazzini's 'Young Italy' movement. He was a brilliant guerrilla leader who fought the French forces sent to overthrow the Roman Republic in 1849. He objected to Cavour's bartering of his native Nice in return for the acquisition of territory and opposed Cavour's approach of orthodox diplomacy and war. In 1860, without Cavour's support, he led his famous Thousand Volunteers on an expedition from Genoa to invade Sicily, where a revolt was in progress. This was the sort of revolutionary activity which Cavour had always deplored. Nevertheless, Garibaldi was able to defeat the army of the King of Naples and free Sicily and Naples in the name of a united Italy.

(e) The Emergence of a Kingdom of Italy (1860–1861)

Cavour seized the initiative by invading the Papal States in September 1860. This was to prevent Garibaldi from attacking Rome, which might lead to the intervention of France and Austria. It was also to prevent an Italian republic as favoured by Mazzini. The Papal army was defeated at Castelfidardo and Victor Emanuel met Garibaldi near Naples, where the latter agreed to hand over his conquests to Victor Emanuel in the cause of unity. Plebiscites confirmed that Naples, Sicily and the Papal states to the east of the Apennines wished to join Piedmont. In 1861, the Kingdom of Italy was proclaimed with Victor Emanuel as King and Cavour as Prime Minister.

(f) Cavour's and Garibaldi's Contribution to Italian Unification

Cavour died in 1861, immediately after the dramatic developments of 1859–1861. He left his royal master as King of a state five times the size of Piedmont. Cavour proved himself to be a brilliant politician, diplomat and statesman. He improved the economy and administration of Piedmont, equipping it to lead the Italian cause; he secured a French alliance so as to defeat Austria; and he enabled Piedmont to expand into Central Italy and acquire Tuscany, Parma and Modena. He did not have a long-range plan to unite Italy. The Plombières agreement did not envisage a united Italy. Rather he took advantage of opportunities as they presented themselves, e.g. the way he used the revolts in the Duchies during the wars of 1859 to ensure their union with Piedmont; he invaded the Papal States, once Garibaldi's success in conquering Sicily and Naples was apparent.

Garibaldi too helped to create a united Italy. His genius for irregular warfare enabled him to acquire Sicily and Naples in 1860. Without his unofficial Expedition of the Thousand, Naples and Sicily would not so easily have been linked to the rest of Italy.

(g) The acquisition of Venetia and Rome

Venetia and Rome were only acquired by the new kingdom as a result of events outside of Italy. In 1866, Italy and Prussia signed a military alliance against Austria and in the war which followed, Prussia's defeat of Austria ensured that Venetia fell into Italian hands. This was despite Italian defeats on land and sea by the Austrians.

Rome was only acquired in 1870 as a result of the withdrawal of the French garrison which had protected the Pope's temporal power.

The Franco-Prussian War of 1870 enabled Italian forces to enter Rome following the withdrawal of the French garrison. This completed the process of Italian unification, though many Italians still remained under Austrian rule. This 'Italia Irredenta' in the Trentino, Trieste and Istria continued to promote ill-feeling between Italy and the Austrian Empire.

(h) The Aftermath of Italian Unity

1. *Foreign help*. It was disillusioning that only foreign help enabled Italy to be united. A French alliance in 1858 was essential to begin the process of unification while Prussia's actions alone ensured the acquisition of Venetia and Rome in 1866 and 1870.

2. *The New Kingdom of Italy*. Italy was poor in that it lacked coal and iron. Its industrial revolution was still in the future. The South was overwhelmingly primitive and illiterate. The arrival of Piedmontese officials and soldiers from the North led to a war between the new authorities and Brigands which lasted till 1865 and claimed more lives than all the battles of the Risorgimento put together.

Essay Questions to Consider

1. Account for the growth of nationalism in Italy between 1815 and 1850.

2. What factors (a) assisted and (b) held back Italian nationalism in the period 1815–1849?

3. Why was there such a growth of national feeling in Italy during the period 1815–1870?

4. Assess the contribution of Cavour in Italy to national unification.

5. "Supreme opportunism was the key to unity." How far would you agree with this statement in relation to Cavour and Italy?

6. "The heart, the sword, and the brain." How well does this describe the part played in Italian unification by Mazzini, Garibaldi and Cavour?

7. "Without the decline of Austria, unification would have been virtually impossible to achieve." How far do you agree in relation to Italy?

8. Why did it take so long for Italy to achieve unification?

9. To what extent was the unification of Italy made possible by foreign intervention?

6. A STUDY OF THE POLITICAL CHARACTER OF THE NEW NATION STATE IN ITALY, 1871–1914, WITH PARTICULAR REFERENCE TO ITS AUTHORITY; THE IMPACT OF NATIONALISM ON THE INTERNATIONAL RELATIONS OF THE NEW STATE

1. Basic Problems of the New Italy

D'Azeglio's remark in 1860, 'Italy is made; now we must make Italians', illustrates the problem facing the rulers of the new Italian Kingdom.

(a) Piedmontisation. The Italian states were annexed by Piedmont, subsequently confirmed by plebiscite. Victor Emanuel II, King of Piedmont, retained his title even though he was the first King of Italy. The Piedmontese constitution of 1848 became the constitution of Italy in 1861.

(b) The Church. The Roman Catholic Church refused official recognition of the new Italian state because the Papacy was not reconciled to the loss of its temporal power. Therefore devout Catholics abstained from voting.

(c) Narrowness of the political system. The mass of the population remained outside the state. Until the extension of the franchise in 1882, less than 2% of the population could vote. This created a gulf between official, 'legal' Italy of the King, Parliament, the politicians and officials and 'real' Italy of the peasant masses. Although compulsory elementary education was introduced in 1887, it could not be immediately enforced and, as late as 1911, 30% of the population was illiterate.

2. The Era of Depretis and Crispi 1876–1896

The Prime Minister for much of the period between 1876–1887 was Agostino Depretis (1813–1887). The system of political management he perfected was attacked as 'trasformismo', whereby the Prime Minister created a majority in Parliament by transforming men of widely different views into colleagues in the same government. This reflected the absence of clearly defined political parties, and the government's dependence on the support of parliamentary deputies, who traded their votes according to the favours they received for their constituencies.

Francesco Crispi (1819–1901), who had attacked this system, became Prime Minister in 1887 and proceeded to operate a new edition of 'trasformismo'. He dominated the years till 1896 but achieved little as he was diverted into a policy of colonial adventures which in the end brought him down.

3. Years of Near-Revolution — 1896–1900

The near-revolutionary crisis in Italy in these years was due to widespread social unrest. The Socialist movement, which Crispi had tried to suppress, supported direct action, including strikes. There were riots due to bad harvests and land hunger. In Milan, in 1898, many civilians were killed by soldiers in street-fighting. In the same year, the government, under General Pelloux, attempted to introduce restrictions on press freedom and on the right to strike. This was a challenge to the Constitution and encountered obstruction in Parliament. In 1900, Pelloux resigned, while in the same year an anarchist assassinated King Humbert in revenge for the dead of Milan.

4. Giolitti and Developments to 1914

Giovanni Giolitti (1842–1928), who was Prime Minister with only brief interruptions between 1903 and 1914, led attempts to include the masses in the political system and to unite the state and nation. He opposed official intervention to break strikes, welcomed the organisation of trade unions and sought the cooperation of the Socialists. In 1912, universal male suffrage for those over 30 was introduced.

Italy made considerable economic progress in these years and the standard of living began to rise. Industrial output increased. However, Italy's problems were not solved: the South remained depressed; agriculture was still starved of investment; emigration remained high and reached a peak of 873,000 in 1913; industrial output remained behind that of Austria-Hungary, which produced three times as much steel as Italy in 1912; social unrest continued: in 1912, the Socialist Congress was dominated by those who opposed collaboration with the government; and in June 1914, during 'Red Week', a Republic was set up in the Romagna and several towns declared themselves independent communes.

5. Foreign Policy 1870–1915

Despite her slender resources and the expense involved, Italy pursued a policy of seeking Great Power status. There was continuing resentment of the Austrian Empire because Italians were still part of that Empire — in Trieste, Austria's main port, and in Istria and the Trentino. Italy also had imperial ambitions and there was intense resentment at the French acquisition of Tunis in 1881. This led to Italy becoming a member of the Triple Alliance in 1882 with Germany and Austria-Hungary.

Italy acquired colonies in the Red Sea from 1882 onwards. This led to attempts to interfere in Abyssinia where, in 1896, Italian forces were defeated with the loss of 6,000 men. This colonial disaster led to the fall of Crispi's administration.

In the years before 1914, Italy moved away from the Triple Alliance, and towards France which, in 1900, promised to support Italy over Libya in return for Italian support for France's interest in Morocco. In 1911, Giolitti bowed to nationalist pressure to acquire Libya from the Turks and, in the ensuing war, Tripoli and Dodecanese Islands were won at enormous strain on the national budget.

In 1914, Italy refused to assist Austria-Hungary against Serbia, on the grounds that Austria had failed to consult with her Italian ally. In 1915, Italy entered the war on the side of the Allies because Britain and France promised Italy substantial gains, at Austria's expense (the Treaty of London), which would have made Italy the dominant power in the Adriatic.

Essay Questions to Consider

1. "A country united in name only." How far would this judgement on Italy during the period 1871–1914?
2. How successful was Italy in dealing with internal political problems between 1871 and 1914?
3. How accurate is it to describe Italy as a united country after 1871?
4. "A period of prolonged crisis." Is this an accurate assessment of the years 1871–1914 in Italy?
5. How successfully did the constitutional monarchy in Italy win popular support in the period 1871–1914?
6. How far did the need for self-preservation influence the international relations of Italy between 1871 and 1914?
7. To what extent did domestic political problems affect the foreign and imperial policy of Italy during the period 1871–1914?
8. How important was imperialism in determining Italy's foreign policy between 1871 and 1914?
9. How far do you accept the view that Italian foreign policy between 1870 and 1914 was dominated by the need to satisfy national pride?
10. Account for Italy's intervention on the side of the Allies in 1915.

7. IN RELATION TO ITALY, THE NATURE OF FASCISM AND THE REASONS FOR ITS VICTORY; THE NATURE OF FASCIST AUTHORITY AND THE USE OF POWER TO 1939

1. The Origins of Fascism

(a) The Failure of Italy's Parliamentary System

Italy's parliamentary system had failed to solve the country's social and political problems. Italy lacked the social unity or economic foundations for effective parliamentary government. The politicians had been unable to make Italy's political system sufficiently strong to ensure its survival. Intransigent Catholicism and Socialism remained outside the parliamentary arena.

(b) The Effects of World War One

The Italian front against Austria proved to be a war of attrition in which Italy's slender resources were found wanting. In 1917, reinforced by German divisions, the Austrians broke through the Italian lines at Caporetto, exposing Venice itself to attack. Anglo-French reinforcements were dispatched to hold the line. Victory was only secured after the internal disintegration of Austria-Hungary in 1918. Six hundred thousand Italians died in the conflict, in which the Italian people had to endure shortages and severe inflation.

(c) Disillusion over the Peace Settlement

Italy failed to secure all the gains promised in the Treaty of London in 1915. She did gain the Brenner frontier, acquiring the Trentino and the South Tyrol as well as the port of Trieste and Istria, but her ambitions clashed with Yugoslav aspirations which were supported by President Wilson. Thus Italy failed to obtain territory which she claimed on the Dalmatian coast or in Albania. Nor was she offered a mandate over any of Germany's African colonies. Discontent led to the unofficial seizure of the disputed city of Fiume by the nationalist D'Annunzio between 1919–1920.

(d) Post-war Instability and Unrest

In 1919–1920, Italy was swept by a wave of social unrest, strikes and disorder. In Turin and Milan, workers occupied factories, while the

83

Socialist party rejected all dealings with non-socialist parties. Many businessmen and industrialists were prepared to support Mussolini's Fascists because they were seen as supporters of strong government. In 1922, the Fascist Squads broke a general strike and ejected socialist councils from office.

(e) The Weakness of Italian Governments and Politicians

There was an absence of cooperation between Liberals, Socialists and the Catholic Popular party, while the Communist Party, formed in 1921, opposed an anti-Fascist Coalition. A series of weak Liberal governments proved unable to provide leadership. Frequently the authorities, including the prefects, police and army commanders, cooperated with the Fascists. Politicians like Giolitti tried to work with the Fascists and give them a share of power. In the 1921 elections, in an alliance with Giolitti, 35 Fascists entered Parliament. By now the Fascist movement was a threat to the Liberal state and constitution.

In 1922, Mussolini threatened to seize power and planned a march on Rome. Although the government of Facta did take precautions and was prepared to proclaim a state of siege, in the end the King refused to sign the order imposing martial law and invited Mussolini to become Prime Minister.

(f) Mussolini's Oratory and the Fascist Movement

Mussolini, who was a journalist by profession, was an effective propagandist. After being expelled from the Socialist party for advocating Italy's entry into the War in 1915, he acquired his own paper, Il Popolo d'Italia. He attracted support from all those discontented by the weakness and failures of Italian governments. He proposed action to heal Italy's divisions and attacked all other parties as discredited. He successfully played on fears of Bolshevism and used his Fascist Squads to break strikes and attack socialists.

2. Mussolini in Power (1922–1943)

Mussolini coined the word 'totalitarian' to describe the Fascist state. He was able to establish a one-party state and a personality cult, though the totalitarian state was never as comprehensive in Italy as the systems established under Hitler and Stalin.

Destruction of Opposition

The Fascist Party soon established its grip on the civil service, judiciary and on local government. The Fascist Squads were transformed into a militia under Mussolini's personal control. Also responsible to the Duce was a Fascist Grand Council which contained the leading Fascist members.

In 1923, Mussolini persuaded Parliament to change the electoral system so that a party with 25% of the poll secured two thirds of the seats. In the 1924 elections, the government secured the necessary votes to enable its list of candidates to be elected and so to dominate Parliament.

After the murder of the outspoken Socialist deputy, Giacomo Matteotti in 1924, most of the non-Fascist deputies withdrew from Parliament. Mussolini proceeded to ban strikes and all non-Fascist political parties. From 1928, all parliamentary candidates had to be approved by the Fascist Grand Council before being submitted to the electorate for approval. The Press was effectively controlled. Mussolini's role as Duce ensured his domination of government. The slogans 'Mussolini is always Right' and 'Believe, Obey, Fight' were endlessly repeated.

3. **The Limits of Totalitarian Rule**

   (a) The Crown survived and so Mussolini never became Head of State in the way Hitler did in 1934.

   (b) The Roman Catholic Church secured recognition of its position in 1929 when Mussolini and the Pope signed the Lateran Agreements, which recognised the Pope as the ruler of the Vatican City, and ensured for the Church control over Italy's marriage laws and of religious instruction in schools.

   (c) Italian Fascism is associated with the idea of the Corporate State. This was supposed to be a new organisation of society and of the economy to replace class conflict with corporations for each branch of economic activity. These corporations were to regulate production, labour relations and social welfare and represented both employers and workers. In 1939, the Chamber of Deputies itself was replaced by a Chamber of Corporations. In practice, however, the corporations were both inefficient and corrupt. They favoured employers and landowners at the expense of workers and peasants.

Essay Questions to Consider

1. Assess the importance of economic factors in the rise to power of the Fascist party in Italy between 1918 and 1924.

2. "The part played by the leader was decisive in the rise to power of Fascist parties." Discuss this judgement with reference to Italy between 1918 and 1923.

3. How far was the achievement of power by Fascists in Italy due to the absence of strong central government?

4. To what extent can Mussolini's rise to power be explained by the weakness of democracy in Italy?

5. Why did Italy become a Fascist state?

6. How effectively did Fascist rule in Italy solve the problems which had brought Mussolini to power?

7. Assess the impact of Fascist rule on the people of Italy up to 1939?

8. How far did the Fascist state depend on fear rather than popular support for its survival? Discuss with reference to Italy between the wars.

9. "Mussolini's domestic achievements can be described at best as superficial." Discuss.

10. "To maintain its authority, Fascism relied on propaganda rather than on solid achievement." How far would you agree, with reference to Italy up to 1939?

11. How exaggerated was the claim that Mussolini "solved the economic and social problems of Italy"?

SECTION C
SPECIAL TOPIC

APPEASEMENT AND THE
ROAD TO WAR, TO 1939

1. **FASCIST IDEOLOGY AND ITS APPLICATION TO THE FOREIGN POLICY OF ITALY FROM 1933; THE EUROPEAN REPERCUSSIONS OF ITALIAN AMBITIONS IN ABYSSINIA; THE FAILURE OF THE LEAGUE OF NATIONS SANCTIONS; THE HOARE-LAVAL PACT, 1935**

Mussolini and Italian Foreign Policy in the 1930s

Outline of Events

1934 — Attempted Nazi Putsch in Austria; Italian troops moved to the Brenner Pass to deter Anschluss.

1935 (April) — At the Stresa Conference, Mussolini united with Britain and France to condemn Hitler's action in repudiating the military clauses of the Treaty of Versailles.

1935 (October) — Italian invasion of Abyssinia from Eritrea; the League of Nations imposed economic sanctions against Italy.

1935 (December) — Hoare-Laval Pact.

1936 (March) — Taking advantage of the Western Powers' preoccupation with the Abyssinian War, Hitler remilitarised the Rhineland.

1936 (May) — Addis Ababa, capital of Abyssinia, fell to Italian forces.

1936–1939 — Italian intervention to assist General Franco in the Spanish Civil War.

1936 (October) — Rome-Berlin Axis.

1937 — Anti-Comintern Pact with Germany and Japan to present a united front against Bolshevism.

1938 (March) — Germany occupied Austria without Italian opposition.

1938 (September) — Mussolini acted as mediator at the Munich Conference.

1939 (April) — Italian forces occupied Albania.

1939 (May) — Pact of Steel committed Germany and Italy to mutual support in a war.

1940 (June) — After Germany's victories, Mussolini declared war on Britain and France.

Italian Foreign Policy Between the Wars

Whereas in 1915 Italy entered the war on the side of the Allies, in 1940 she supported Germany by attacking France. Though on the winning side in 1918–1919, Italy became a 'revisionist' power, discontented with her gains from the peace settlement.

Mussolini profited enormously from Nationalist discontent. He offered a strong government at home as a platform for a vigorous foreign policy. Italy's international revisionism suggested some arrangement with Germany to challenge Anglo-French hegemony. A German Alliance was achieved in the 1930s.

Hitler never threatened Italy's possession of the Alto Adige or South Tyrol. This was won in 1919 and contained 200,000 German-speaking former Habsburg subjects. It brought Italy's border up to the strategic Brenner Pass. To secure the South Tyrol, Italian interests required an independent and weak Austria, while Hitler's programme envisaged 'Anschluss'.

Mussolini patronised Dolfuss, the Austrian Chancellor, who in 1934 attacked the Socialists and established an authoritarian regime. In the same year, Dolfuss was murdered by Austrian Nazis in a coup intended to bring about Anschluss. This led Mussolini to threaten military intervention in Austria. Hitler did not abandon the goal of Anschluss but set out to conciliate Italy.

At first Mussolini sided with the Western Powers against Hitler. At the Stresa Conference, in 1935, Britain, France and Italy lined up in favour of the Treaty of Versailles and against German rearmament. They also reaffirmed their support for the independence of Austria.

It was the Abyssinian crisis which destroyed the trust between Italy and the Western Powers. The conquest of Abyssinia (1935–1936) was the result of the Fascist policy of expansion and conquest and the Italian desire for colonies. Italian Nationalists had never forgotten Italy's defeat by Abyssinian tribesmen in the battle of Adowa in 1896. Placed alongside Italian Eritrea and Somaliland, Abyssinia was seen as an Italian reserve. Fascism needed the prestige of a military victory. Mussolini's view was that 'a nation, to remain healthy, should make war every 25 years'.

However, Abyssinia was a member of the League of Nations and the League condemned Italy as an aggressor following the invasion launched in October 1935. It imposed economic sanctions: all League members were to ban imports from Italy, loans to Italy and the supply of war materials. However, the sanctions excluded oil and coal, essential in waging war. Moreover, in December, the British and French foreign ministers, Samuel Hoare and Pierre Laval, put forward a compromise proposal giving Italy over a half of Abyssinia if Mussolini agreed to stop the war. When the news of this leaked out, there was a storm of protest in Britain, as it seemed a betrayal of the Abyssinians and a surrender to aggression. Hoare was forced to resign but the damage to the League's credibility was long-lasting. It showed the extent to which the British and French governments were afraid of upsetting Mussolini, whom they saw as an ally against Hitler. Indeed, the German army was able to take advantage of the Abyssinian crisis by reoccupying the Rhineland, contrary to the treaty of Versailles.

Undeterred by the League, the Italians used aerial bombardment and poison gas to subdue the Abyssinians. By May 1936, their forces occupied Addis Ababa. Mussolini defiantly proclaimed the existence of the Italian Empire. When the Abyssinian Emperor Haile Selassie came to Geneva, to protest at the League of Nations, he was greeted by booing from Italian journalists. Italy had successfully defied the League of Nations in a war of aggression.

Mussolini increasingly inclined to the view that Britain and France were 'decadent' and feeble. Moreover, the Anglo-French campaign to stave off foreign intervention in the Spanish Civil War was ineffectual, and Mussolini provided substantial assistance to the anti-Republican cause in Spain.

When, in 1936, the Rome-Berlin Axis was announced, Austria's independence was compromised. Austria increasingly fell under the German orbit and, in 1938, Anschluss was accomplished without Italian interference. Under German influence, racial anti-semitic laws on the Nazi model were introduced in Italy in 1938. In the same year there were increased demands for the French possessions of Tunis, Corsica, Nice and Savoy. To convert the Mediterranean into an Italian lake (Mare Nostrum) the British would have to give up Gibraltar, Malta and Suez. In 1939, the Pact of Steel between Germany and Italy was a formal military alliance, committing both to mutual support in a war.

In fact, Italy remained neutral when Germany attacked Poland in September 1939. The fact was that Italy was not ready for a major war. The Abyssinian war and involvement in Spain had seriously drained Italian resources and Italy lacked tanks and modern artillery. Yet Mussolini found 'non-belligerence' intolerable for a fascist state and intervened following the German invasion of France in 1940.

2. THE SPANISH CIVIL WAR

A Chronology of the main political events, before and during the Civil War.

1923 — Military rebellion by General Primo de Rivera overthrew the Parliamentary system.

1925 — Spanish military victory in Morocco.

1930 — Primo resigned.

1931 — Municipal elections saw the defeat of Monarchist candidates in the large towns. As a result King Alfonso XIII went into exile.

1931–36 — Spain was a Republic.

1932 — Autonomy granted to Catalonia provoked a military rebellion by General Sanjurjo.

1933 — Conservative victory in the General Election.

1935 — Formation of the Popular Front of Republicans, Socialists, Communists and Anarchists.

1936 — Electoral victory of the Popular Front (February).
In July, a military rebellion by Generals Franco, Mola and Sanjurjo was launched from Spanish Morocco. These rebels formed the Nationalist forces in the ensuing Civil War.
November: Franco, who became Head of State on the Nationalist side, failed to take Madrid. The International Brigades (Left-wing volunteers from many countries) arrived to assist the Republicans, the elected government.
December: By the end of 1936, Franco controlled more than half of Spain, but not including Madrid, Bilbao or Barcelona.

1937 — Nationalist offensive, including Italian troops, was held at Guadalajara, outside Madrid (March).
April: Franco's Northern offensive. Guernica bombed by the German Condor Legion.
June: Bilbao fell to the Nationalists; the Basque country was now in Nationalist hands. They controlled two thirds of Spain.

1938 — April: The Nationalists reached the Mediterranean, following an offensive aimed at cutting the Republican territory in two.
December: With the use of German artillery, the Nationalists triumphed over the Republican forces in Catalonia.

1939 — January: Nationalist forces entered Barcelona.
March: The surrender of Madrid.

The Spanish Civil War

The Origins of the War

The Spanish Civil War of 1936–1939 had its origins in the political, social and economic divisions in Spain. The country lacked political stability and the army frequently intervened in government. From 1923–1930, Spain was ruled by the military dictator General Primo de Rivera. This regime collapsed due to the strains of the world economic crisis which began in 1929.

There followed a period of bitter hostility between the Left and the Right in Spain, culminating in the outbreak of the Civil War. In 1931, the King abdicated after the Republicans won local elections. From 1931–1936 Spain was a Republic. The Republic was dominated by the Left from 1931–1933. Major reforms were introduced, including autonomy to Catalonia, a law to reduce large landholdings in the interests of the landless peasantry and measures to reduce the power of the army and the Church. These measures alarmed the Church, the army, the landowners and industrialists. In the General Election of 1933, the Right won power and tried to dismantle the previous reforms. However, in the elections of February 1936, a Popular Front of Left and moderate parties won. It was supported by Catalan and Basque nationalists who wanted home rule for their provinces. This produced an Army rebellion with Spain polarised between a National Front (monarchists, landowners, the army, the Church and the employers) and the Republican Popular Front Government (Liberals, trade unions, Socialists, Communists and Anarchists).

Outside Intervention in the Civil War

The Spanish Civil War lasted nearly three years; it was a ferocious conflict which had a devastating effect on Spain. Had the Spaniards been left to themselves, the two sides were not unevenly matched. However, from the start the war was marked by outside intervention.

The Nationalists would probably not have been able to win the war without assistance from Mussolini's Italy and Hitler's Germany. Mussolini's motives for intervention included the desire to expand the Fascist creed, enhance the prestige of his regime and strengthen Italy's Mediterranean position. Hitler too saw the war as an anti-Bolshevik crusade. He also regarded Spain as a testing ground for Germany's new armaments. In all, Italy provided over 50,000 ground troops, 950 tanks, over 700 aircraft and 90-odd warships. Germany provided 16,000 military advisers and effective airforce units. This Fascist support was of great importance to the Nationalist forces. German and Italian aircraft transported Franco's troops from Morocco to southern Spain at the beginning of the war. In 1937, Italian supplies kept the Nationalists fighting after Republican successes. In 1939, another flow of armaments made it possible for Franco to crush Catalonia. The Republic too received outside help, though it was more intermittent. Stalin sent valuable military equipment, including 1000 aircraft, 200 tanks and the services of military advisers. Yet Soviet resources were limited. Stalin had no intention of wasting his resources in the face of the threat to the U.S.S.R. from Germany and Japan. He also took advantage of the Republic's control of Spain's gold reserves, which were used to purchase the Soviet supplies. After 1938, when it was clear that the Republic would lose the war, Stalin withdrew his assistance. He was never as committed to the conflict as Hitler and Mussolini.

The Spanish government was forced to rely on the services of the International Brigades. These were volunteers from various countries. They were left-wing sympathisers and provided a morale-booster to the Republicans, e.g., in 1937 they assisted in the successful defence of Madrid. Organised by the Communists, they were, however, no match for the superior equipment, training and discipline of the Nationalist forces.

The attitude of Britain and France was crucial to the outcome of the war. Although France had a Popular Front government in 1936, it was unable to extend aid to its Spanish counterpart due to right-wing hostility within France. It also had to take account of British hostility to intervention. The mainly Conservative government in London wanted to avoid a confrontation with Italy and Germany. There was also a distaste for Stalin's intervention and for the strong left-wing influence on the Republican side. Britain and France sponsored the Non-Intervention Committee which aimed to prevent outside help reaching either side. What this did was to deny the Spanish government supplies from the outside world. It was unable to prevent German and Italian supplies reaching the Nationalists. Hitler and Mussolini ignored the Non-Intervention Committee. Indeed, the British government wanted the war in Spain to be over as soon as possible, and that meant victory for Franco.

Finally the Nationalist victory was also the result of the greater cohesion of the Nationalist forces which were skilfully led by Franco. He welded together the Monarchists, Fascists, Conservatives and the army into an effective coalition. By contrast, the Republicans were riven by disunity. There was tension between Communists and Anarchists and a general factiousness which weakened the Republican side.

3.   APPEASEMENT IN ACTION:
THE REOCCUPATION OF THE RHINELAND

Hitler's Initial Moves in Foreign and Military Policy

In his rise to power, Hitler attacked the alleged discrimination against Germans in the Versailles Treaty. He complained that Germany was unilaterally forced to disarm, that self-determination seemed to have been applied to everybody but the Germans, and that Germany had been unfairly saddled with War Guilt.

When he came to power, he avoided overtly aggressive moves. He expressed a willingness to cooperate with a general disarmament, if only other nations would disarm to German levels. In 1933, he withdrew Germany from the League of Nations and its Disarmament Conference, claiming France and the other Powers refused to accept parity with Germany.

In 1935, he re-introduced conscription and revealed the existence of the air-force. Despite this rearmament, which was contrary to the Treaty of Versailles, Britain came to an agreement with Germany, without consulting France, that Germany could build up to 35% of Britain's naval strength (the Anglo-German Naval Agreement). 1935 saw what Hitler regarded as another blow to the Treaty of Versailles — the return to Germany of the Saar, an important coal-producing area, following a plebiscite. This German-speaking area overwhelmingly voted for reunion with Germany.

In March 1936, Hitler achieved his boldest move to date, the re-entry of German troops into the demilitarised Rhineland. The Treaty of Versailles had imposed a demilitarised status on this part of Germany which bordered France and Belgium. Article 42 of the Treaty stated, 'Germany is forbidden to maintain or construct any fortifications either on the left bank of the Rhine, or on the right bank to the west of a line drawn 50 km to the east.' The demilitarised zone had been instituted in 1919 to deter Germany from a war of aggression. In the event of war, this part of Germany would fall immediately as a hostage into French hands. The Treaty of Locarno (1925) had confirmed its status.

Hitler's Reoccupation was a unilateral repudiation of a Treaty obligation. He justified it by claiming that the Franco-Soviet Pact for mutual assistance, ratified by the French Parliament in February 1936, was a breach of the Treaty of Locarno. Hitler had chosen his moment well, for Italy was then at loggerheads with Britain and France over Abyssinia. He claimed he only

93

sought equality with other Powers and affirmed 'Germany had no territorial demands to make in Europe.'

The success of Hitler's move seemed to confirm his judgement. The German General Staff had expected France to respond with action. They knew that they could not hold out for long against a British and French attack and had opposed Hitler's order. His success further strengthened his power over the generals.

The Council of the League of Nations condemned Germany as guilty of a breach of her treaty obligations. The British and French governments also publicly deplored the disregard of treaty requirements. Yet no effective action was taken. In Britain, the public, holding feelings of guilt over the Versailles Treaty, were soothed with the view that the Germans were only 'going into their back-garden'.

The French government refused to take action without British support and the British government refused to commit itself, citing as a reason British military weakness. French opinion at this critical time was divided between the supporters of the Right and the Popular Front of Socialists, Communists and radicals. As a result, national unity was threatened and French opinion seemed paralysed in the face of German aggression.

The whole affair was a major set-back for France. French security was dependent on a demilitarised Rhineland. France's network of alliances with east European states was devalued once Hitler had fortified the Rhineland, which was no longer an easy French conquest in the event of German aggression against Poland or Czechoslovakia. Increasingly, France became dependent on Britain. French defensive mentality is seen in the reliance placed on the Maginot Line of fortifications on the Franco-German border.

As for Belgium, it had regarded the demilitarised zone as a safeguard against a German attack. It now felt vulnerable to such an attack. Britain and France were faced with the prospect of war. Britain began to rearm and reaffirmed its obligations under the Treaty of Locarno, namely that Britain would come to the help of France and Belgium if they were attacked by Germany.

4. THE GERMAN ANNEXATION OF AUSTRIA

The Road to Anschluss: an Outline of Events

1866 — Bismarck excluded Austria from Germany, in the process of German unification (Kleindeutschland).

1889 — Hitler was born in Austria. He lived in Vienna from 1909–1913, where he absorbed anti-semitic prejudices.

1918 — Break-up of Austro-Hungarian Empire; Austria became a small entirely German-speaking Republic.

1919 — Treaties of Versailles and St. Germain forbade the union of Germany and Austria.

1925 — In *Mein Kampf*, Hitler stated "German-Austria must be restored to the great German motherland . . . people of the same blood should be in the same Reich."

1931 — Following the economic slump, the main Austrian bank, the Creditanstalt, collapsed.

1932 — Dolfuss became Austrian Chancellor.

1934 — Dolfuss was murdered in a failed coup by the Austrian Nazis. Italian troops moved to the Austrian border to deter a German invasion.

1936 — Rome-Berlin Axis; Mussolini gave up his role as protector of Austria; German-Austrian agreement.

1937 — Hitler told his generals that the independence of Austria and Czechoslovakia must be ended as soon as possible.

1938 — February: The Austrian Chancellor, Schuschnigg, visited Hitler at Berchtesgaden where he was bullied into virtually surrendering Austrian independence.

March 9: in an act of defiance, Schuschnigg announced a Plebiscite on Austrian independence.

March 10: Hitler demanded the Plebiscite be called off and that Schuschnigg should resign.

March 11: On secret German orders, Austrian request sent for German intervention to restore order.

March 12: German troops entered Austria unopposed.

March 13: Hitler declared the union of his native Austria with the German Reich.

April 10: Hitler held a plebiscite in Austria and an overwhelming vote for Anschluss was recorded.

Austria: The Road to Anschluss

Austria, formerly the centre of a great multi-national Empire, was reduced in 1918 to a small republic of German speakers. Many 'German-Austrians' were excluded from Austria, namely in the Sudeten area of Czechoslovakia and in the South Tyrol under Italy.

The victorious Allies insisted on an absolute ban on the union of Germany and Austria (Anschluss). Austria therefore seemed an artificial creation and the new Republic had to be rescued from bankruptcy by the League of Nations in 1922. There was considerable internal strife betwen the Socialists and Conservative interests. Fascist Italy aided anti-Socialist groups.

Dolfuss, the Austrian Chancellor (1932–1934), was supported by Mussolini in dissolving Parliament, and curbing both the Socialists and the Austrian Nazis. In a brief Civil War in 1934, his government suppressed the Socialists. However the greatest threat he faced was from the Austrian Nazis.

Hitler wanted the local Nazis to overthrow the Dolfuss regime, as a prelude to Anschluss. When Dolfuss banned the Austrian Nazi party, German propaganda against Austria was stepped up. This culminated in a coup organised by the Austrian Nazis in which Dolfuss was murdered but which failed to shake the loyalty of the police and army. Mussolini replied to the putsch by moving Italian forces up to the Brenner Pass.

Hitler had, for the moment, to accept these developments but he still sought to undermine Austrian independence. Instead of force, he now used German influence to undermine the Austrian will to resist.

Dolfuss' successor as Chancellor was Schuschnigg, who tried to preserve Austria's existence. His policy was to avoid giving the Germans a pretext for intervention. What undermined Austria's position was Mussolini's withdrawal from the role of the protector of Austria. This occurred because of the invasion of Abyssinia which was opposed by Britain and France. In 1936, Italy did not resist an agreement between the Austrian and German governments. This allowed Nazi newspapers to appear and Nazi supporters to be appointed to official positions. Austria's foreign policy was to be parallel to that of Germany. It was as if Austria was a satellite of Nazi Germany. In 1937, Hitler told his generals that Austria and Czechoslovakia were soon to be liquidated.

In February 1938, Schuschnigg visited Hitler, ostensibly to discuss 'improvements in the working of the July (1936) agreement'. However, Hitler stormed at the Austrian Chancellor in a threatening manner, demanding the appointment of the Austrian Nazi, Seyss-Inquart, as Minister of the Interior. He further demanded the lifting of all restrictions on Nazi activity.

It seemed that Germany was about to take over Austria. On his return, Schuschnigg made a final gesture. On 9th March, he announced a plebiscite for or against 'a free and German, independent and social, Christian and united Austria.' Hitler was furious, for if Schuschnigg won, it would postpone the Anschluss. The plebiscite was to be held on 13th March. On 10th March, Hitler ordered preparations for an invasion and demanded that the plebiscite be called off. Schuschnigg knew that he could get no help from Italy, France or Britain. The plebiscite was abandoned and Schuschnigg resigned. Seyss-Inquart was told to request German aid and, on 12th March, German troops entered Austria unopposed.

On 12th March, Hitler declared at Linz in Austria, 'Austria is a province of the German Reich.' The collapse of Austria was the result of the West's policy of appeasement and of Mussolini's friendship with Hitler. On 10th April, Hitler held his own plebiscite in Austria. By then there was general acquiesence in Austria to the Anschluss and Hitler received a massive 'Yes'.

5. THE CRISES OVER CZECHOSLOVAKIA

Czechoslovakia after 1918: An Outline of Events

1918–1919 — Czechoslovakia was formed out of the territory of the Habsburg Empire. It consisted of Bohemia and Moravia (the home of the Czechs) and Slovakia (the land of the Slovaks).

1921 — The 'Little Entente' of Czechoslovakia, Yugoslavia and Romania, supported by France, to uphold the peace settlement.

1925 — Franco-Czech Treaty of mutual assistance.

1935 — Franco-Soviet Pact involved a Treaty binding the U.S.S.R. to support French action in defence of Czechoslovakia.

1937 — Hitler told his generals that he aimed to overthrow Austria and Czechoslovakia as soon as possible. He identified Britain and France as obstacles to his ambition to acquire Lebensraum in Eastern Europe.

1938 — Hitler took advantage of the grievances of the Sudeten Germans against the Czechs.
7th September: *The Times* suggested the cession of the Sudetenland to Germany as a solution to the crisis.
15th September: Chamberlain visited Hitler at Berchtesgaden. As a result pressure was put on the Czechs to surrender the Sudetenland to Germany.
22nd September: Chamberlain visited Hitler again at Godesberg. Chamberlain rejected Hitler's demand that the Sudetenland be handed over to Germany at once.
28th September: Four-Power talks of Britain, France, Italy and Germany at Munich. Agreement reached involving the Czech surrender of the Sudetenland to Germany.

1939 — March: Germany occupies the remainder of Bohemia and Moravia.

Czechoslovakia and the Appeasement of Germany

Czechoslovakia was the most successful of the 'new' states born in 1918, from both an economic and democratic point of view. Yet, after only 20 years, its independent existence was destroyed by Hitler's Germany.

The two Slav peoples, Czech and Slovak, came together in the new state which also contained substantial national minorities — over three million German speakers and smaller numbers of Hungarians, Ukrainians and Poles. Czechoslovakia had a well-developed industrial economy in the west of the country. This relative economic prosperity made democracy possible, in contrast to the other states of Eastern Europe. Czech governments under Presidents Masaryk (1918–1935) and Benes (1935–1938) were strong supporters of the League of Nations and the idea of collective security.

The greatest threat to the Czech state came from the Sudeten Germans and from Hitler's Germany. These Germans had not been part of Germany but, like the Czechs, subjects of the pre-war Habsburg Empire. They were unreconciled to their inclusion in the new state, though the Sudetenland gave the country a secure and defendable frontier. German grievances in the Sudetenland were sharpened by the slump of the 1930s which caused considerable unemployment. Konrad Henlein's Sudeten German Party attracted support from most of the German voters. Hitler provided the party with political and financial support. After the Anschluss in 1938, it was obvious that the Sudeten German problem was next on the agenda. Since the reoccupation of the Rhineland in 1936, Czechoslovakia's security was threatened because France was no longer such a credible deterrent to Germany.

In May 1938, Hitler issued the following military order: 'It is my unalterable decision to smash Czechoslovakia by military action in the near future.' He hoped to launch a decisive attack before any possible intervention by the Western Powers. He was able to manufacture a crisis by means of the discontent of the Sudeten Germans. Henlein was under instructions to 'always demand so much that we can never be satisfied'.

Although the Czechs had an efficient army and formidable frontier defences, Hitler was confident that the Western Powers would not risk starting a war over the issue of the Sudetenland. Equally the Czech government believed that France and Britain would support them in resisting the Germans. When the Czechs took firm action against Henlein's party, Hitler portrayed the

Sudenten Germans as the victims of oppression. Moreover, it was the policy of the British P.M. Neville Chamberlain to accommodate Hitler's demands as part of a settlement of European disputes to preserve peace. In September, *The Times*, which expressed influential opinion, proposed giving Germany the Sudetenland as a solution. To prevent unilateral German action, Chamberlain decided to solve the Czech crisis by personal contact with Hitler. On 15th September, he flew to Germany and met Hitler at Berchtesgaden. Here the P.M. was prepared, in principle, to concede the surrender of the Sudetenland to Germany. He also spoke of the need to consult his Cabinet and the French.

On his return he persuaded the Cabinet and the French, who were allies of the Czechs, to agree. On 22nd September, having obtained the reluctant concurrence of the Czechs, he flew to see Hitler for a second meeting — this time to Godesberg. Here Hitler demanded the immediate Czech surrender of the Sudetenland without any delay. Chamberlain reproached Hitler for his failure to reciprocate the British efforts to secure peace. It seemed that Hitler was determined to invade Czechoslovakia. Hitler relented only to the extent of agreeing to postpone his deadline for an invasion to 1st October.

Chamberlain was deeply depressed at the thought of war and was concerned at British vulnerability to German aerial attack. This explains his acceptance of an invitation to a four-Power Conference at Munich (29th to 30th September) at which Great Britain, France, Italy and Germany agreed to the German occupation of the Sudetenland between 1st to 10th October. Neither the Czechs nor the Soviet Union were consulted. The Czechs were faced with acceptance or single combat with Germany. Chamberlain persuaded Hitler to sign a joint-declaration after the signature of the Munich agreement: 'We (i.e. Hitler and Chamberlain) regard the (Munich) agreement and the Anglo-German naval agreement as symbolic of the desire of our two peoples never to go to war with one another again.'

Hitler regarded this agreement as of no importance. Nor was he content with the Munich agreement, since he had wanted the destruction of the Czech state. As he said, 'That fellow Chamberlain has spoiled my entry into Prague.' For the Czechs, the Munich agreement was a tragedy: the country's defences were given up without a fight, the army was demoralised and the will to resist was gone.

The initial reaction of British and French public opinion was favourable: it seemed as if war had been avoided. Chamberlain hoped that Munich would lead to a general settlement of European disputes. On his return home, he claimed he brought back 'peace for our time' and 'peace with honour'. Chamberlain was, in private, less confident and while he hoped Hitler would settle for a permanent peace, he did press ahead with rearmament. In the long run, Munich was to be a disaster for Chamberlain's reputation. The very name Munich has become associated with the cowardly surrender of principle.

The success of the Sudeten Germans encouraged other separatists in Czechoslovakia. After the Munich Conference, Poland and Hungary, with German support, annexed parts of Czechoslovakia which they claimed. Neither Britain nor France were consulted. Hitler's objective remained the complete destruction of the Czech state. In March 1939, under German pressure, Slovakia declared its independence and German troops occupied Bohemia and Moravia, which was declared a German Protectorate.

Thus Czechoslovakia had been dismembered and partitioned. This was the first territory which Hitler acquired with a non-German population. There was anger and dismay in Britain at Hitler's breach of the Munich agreement. On 31st March, in a reversal of policy, Britain guaranteed Poland's independence. Poland seemed likely to be Germany's next victim. In June, conscription for men over twenty was introduced. The partition of Czechoslovakia had caused Britain to abandon the policy of appeasement.

6. THE POLISH CRISIS AND THE EVENTS LEADING TO
THE OUTBREAK OF WAR IN SEPTEMBER 1939

Poland between the Wars: An Outline of Events

1918 — Poland, having been partitioned in the 18th century by Austria, Prussia and Russia, regained its independence with the defeat of the partitioning Powers.

1920–1921 — Polish-Soviet War.

1921 — Treaty of Riga with the Bolshevik regime in Russia settled Poland's eastern border to Russia's disadvantage.

1925 — France and Poland signed an alliance.

1934 — Poland concluded a Non-aggression Pact with Nazi Germany.

1939 — 31st March: Britain gave Poland a guarantee of her independence.
23rd August: Nazi-Soviet Pact.
1st September: Germany attacked Poland.
3rd September: Britain and France declared war on Germany.
17th September: U.S.S.R. invaded Poland, which was partitioned between Germany and the U.S.S.R.

Poland between the Wars

Polish Independence

In the 18th century, Poland had been partitioned by Austria, Prussia and Russia. Polish independence in 1918 was the result of the defeat of the German, Austrian and Russian Empires. In January 1918, President Wilson included the setting-up of an independent Poland as one of his 14 Point War Aims. Marshal Pilsudski, who had fought the Russians in the First World War, became Head of State and commander of the armed forces.

Poland's Borders

Poland obtained from Germany a Corridor of land giving her an outlet to the Baltic Sea. This split Germany from her province of East Prussia. The port city of Danzig, mostly German in population, was made a Free City under the protection of the League of Nations and in a customs union with Poland. Poland's eastern border was only settled after a Polish-Soviet war in 1920–1921. This fixed the eastern border in Poland's favour.

The Ethnic Make-Up of Poland

Between the wars, Poland contained large national minorities — Ukrainians, Byelorussians, Jews, Germans and Lithuanians. A census in 1931 found that less than 70% of the population was Polish. Poland therefore contained resentful national minorities, including nearly three quarters of a million Germans.

Poland's Vulnerability

German nationalist opinion regarded Polish independence as a disaster to be ended at the first opportunity. The U.S.S.R. too was hostile to Poland. Though Poland had a treaty of alliance with France, Pilsudski was sceptical of French support and he signed non-aggression pacts with the U.S.S.R. in 1932 and with Nazi Germany in 1934. In fact, Poland's armed forces were too weak to sustain a policy of 'balancing' Poland's two historic enemies. There were insufficient tanks, planes and anti-aircraft guns.

The Polish Crisis and the Outbreak of War

Poland benefitted from Hitler's dismemberment of Czechoslovakia by occupying the Polish-speaking Teschen area of Czechoslovakia in 1938. However, the demise of the Czech state in 1939 meant that Poland was Hitler's next victim. After the German occupation of Bohemia and Moravia in March 1939, Britain and France gave Poland a formal guarantee of her independence.

This did not deter Hitler, who renounced his 1934 Pact with Poland. He demanded the 'return' of Danzig to the Reich and territorial rights in the Polish Corridor for access to East Prussia. The Polish government resisted these demands. They were not going to follow the Czech example of negotiating over borders: Danzig would not save Polish independence. Indeed, Hitler, in May, addressed senior officers to the effect that Danzig was not 'at stake for us; it is a matter of expanding our living space in the east.'

In 1939, due to the crisis over Poland, both the Western Powers and Germany courted Stalin. Without a Russian alliance, Britain and France could not give Poland any effective military assistance. Yet they were suspicious of Stalin and showed little urgency in talks with him. These negotiations collapsed in August over Poland's reluctance to allow Soviet troops to cross her territory in the event of a war. Accordingly, Stalin opted for an agreement with Hitler. In May, Litvinov, associated with the policy of collective security, was replaced as Foreign Minister by Molotov, a member of the Politburo. In August, Ribbentrop, the German Foreign Minister, arrived in Moscow, where a German-Soviet non-aggression pact was signed.

This provided that neither would attack the other and in a secret protocol Poland was divided between them. Stalin was also given the predominant influence in Finland, Estonia and Latvia. This agreement gave Stalin security from attack and Hitler the necessary safeguard prior to unleashing his attack on Poland. No doubt Hitler hoped that the Western Powers would be so stunned by the Nazi-Soviet Pact that they would lose the heart for war. Yet the British and French governments reaffirmed their guarantee to Poland. There was to be no repeat of Munich.

Eight days after the Nazi-Soviet Pact on 1st September, Germany invaded Poland. So rapid was the German advance that, on 17th September, the Russians invaded Poland to occupy their share. Poland's independence was therefore extinguished by her two historic enemies.

7. THE POLICY OF APPEASEMENT

In the 1930s, the policy of appeasement was followed by British and French governments. It involved the attempt to conciliate the European Dictators, as opposed to standing up to them and resisting their ambitions. Two examples from 1935 were the Hoare-Laval Pact to appease Mussolini by the partition of Abyssinia and the Anglo-German Naval Agreement which permitted a German Navy, despite the express prohibition of the Versailles Treaty.

Appeasement is especially associated with Neville Chamberlain, the British P.M. (1937–1940). He was determined to bring peace to Europe, not through the by then discredited League of Nations but by means of personal diplomacy and agreement.

Verdicts on Appeasement

This policy was roundly condemned, once Britain was fighting for its survival in 1940 against Nazi Germany. It has become synonymous with moral weakness and a lack of willpower. More recently, a less harsh view of appeasement has been put forward. British opinion was pacific and inclined to give Germany the benefit of the doubt. Appeasement reflected the national mood that the Treaty of Versailles was unfair to Germany. There was no desire to go to war over the reoccupation of the Rhineland or the Sudeten areas of Czechoslovakia. In particular, it has been asserted that Chamberlain was a strong Prime Minister who helped to save Britain from defeat in World War 2. He gave Britain sufficient time in which to accelerate essential rearmament.

Points about Appeasement

1. There was a general belief in the 1930s that German grievances over the Treaty of Versailles were reasonable, e.g. the denial of self-determination to Germans in Austria or the Sudetenland; the apparent reasonableness of Hitler's reoccupation of the Rhineland. It was pointed out that Germany could not be expected to endure discrimination while other Powers were armed.

2. There was a widespread revulsion at the thought of war based on the horrors of the First World War and the reality of the Spanish Civil War. In 1933, the Union of Oxford University voted in a celebrated debate

against fighting 'for King and Country'. Labour Party opinion at first opposed rearmament. Public opinion was relieved at the avoidance of war over the Czech problem in 1938.

3.   Appeasement of Hitler gave Britain time to rearm. Britain lacked a large army and she needed to build up her aerial defences. By 1939, Britain was in a better position to fight Germany. The fact was that the Empire was vulnerable to three potential enemies — Germany in Northern Europe, Italy in the Mediterranean and Japan in the Far East. Chamberlain knew that Britain could not face three enemies at once. From 1935, the Chiefs of Staff repeatedly stressed British naval and military weakness. Britain could have done little to help Czechoslovakia in 1938, while the guarantee to Poland in 1939 was more a political than a military move. Britain seemed vulnerable to aerial attack from the Luftwaffe.

4.   There was a widespread dislike and fear of Communism, and Fascism was often portrayed as Europe's best defence against Bolshevism. Cooperation with Stalinist Russia was not easy and the difficulties in the way of an agreement between the Western Powers and the U.S.S.R. in 1939 were to prove insuperable. There was considerable scepticism about the effectiveness of the Soviet army and about Soviet sincerity.

5.   Since 1919, the U.S.A. had abandoned active involvement in European affairs. U.S. intervention in the First World War was seen as an aberration and America reverted to its traditional policy of isolation. Despite its financial and industrial importance, the U.S.A. avoided doing anything substantial in Europe or the Far East. In the 1930s, there was a preoccupation with the Depression, and the affairs of Europe seemed remote from American concerns. The U.S. never became a member of the League of Nations. Chamberlain was aware that there was no possibility of American armed intervention in Europe.

Conclusion

In the end, the policy of appeasement was to fail. Chamberlain was unable to bring about a general settlement in Europe. The outbreak of war was a bitter blow to the Prime Minister. Subsequently, he looked ill at ease as a war leader and resigned the premiership in 1940, following Hitler's rapid military victories against the Low Countries, Denmark and Norway.

The fundamental weakness of appeasement was that it misjudged the nature and aims of Hitler's regime. Hitler was not a 'normal' leader with rational and satisfiable objectives. Although a superb tactician, his long-range objective remained the creation of a racial Empire dominated by the Aryan master-race. He respected no treaty and tore up the Munich agreement in 1939 when he occupied Prague. He would not have been satisfied by the removal of German grievances.

Chamberlain and the appeasers went to the limit in buying off Hitler and Mussolini. More could have been done to secure an agreement with the Soviet Union and there was a lack of urgency about the negotiations between the Western Powers and Stalin in 1939. Hitler correctly perceived that there would be no effective British or French opposition to the extension of German power in Europe. Chamberlain's desire to conciliate Mussolini so enraged Eden, the Foreign Secretary, that he resigned in 1938.

Chamberlain went to almost any lengths to tame Hitler. Although the public were relieved at the Munich agreement, it was left to Churchill to express doubts about British weakness in face of Hitler's demands, 'finding intolerable the sense of our country falling into the power, orbit and influence of Nazi Germany'. More consideration might have been taken of German weaknesses and a strong stand taken against Hitler. The value of the Czech army was ignored and Czechoslovakia was abandoned by the Western Powers to its fate. In 1938, there was an over-estimation of the size of the German armed forces and the amount of destruction the German air-force could inflict on British cities.

Essay Questions on the Special Topic

1. For what reasons were there varying European reactions to the Italian invasion of Abyssinia?

2. "The Hoare–Laval Pact doomed Abyssinia and the League." Do you agree?

3. Examine the reasons for the League of Nations' failure to save Abyssinia from Italian aggression.

4. "Franco's victory was primarily due to German and Italian intervention." Do you agree with this view of the Nationalist victory in the Spanish Civil War?

5. "The adherence of Britain and France to non-intervention sealed the Republic's fate." Does this adequately explain the Republican defeat in the Spanish Civil War?

6. Account for the Nationalist victory in the Spanish Civil War.

7. Explain the failure of Britain and France to prevent German reoccupation of the Rhineland in 1936.

8. Why was there a lack of international opposition to Hitler's reoccupation of the Rhineland in 1936 and the Anschluss in 1938?

9. "As Mussolini's star fell, Hitler's rose." Do you agree this accounts for Italian opposition to Anschluss in 1934 and acceptance of it in 1938?

10. To what extent could Britain and France justify their policy of defending Poland but not Czechoslovakia in 1939?

11. Why did the Second World War break out over Poland but not over Czechoslovakia?

12. To what extent was war between Britain and Germany inevitable after the British guarantee to Poland?

13. Examine the view that it was the policy of Appeasement which was the cause of the Second World War.

14. Why did the German invasion of Poland lead to the outbreak of the Second World War?

15. Why, and with what consequences, did Stalin enter into a pact with Hitler in 1939?

NOTES

NOTES

NOTES

NOTES

Printed by Bell & Bain Ltd., Glasgow, Scotland.